Generalist Social Work Practice in the Wake of Disaster:
September 11 and Beyond

Diane Mirabito, D.S.W.

Caroline Rosenthal, Ph.D.

Co authors

Generalist Social Work Practice in the Wake of Disaster:
September 11 and Beyond

Table of Contents

PART I / INTRODUCTION:
GENERALIST SOCIAL WORK PRACTICE IN THE WAKE OF DISASTER

Table of Contents

PART II / THEORETICAL FOUNDATIONS: GENERALIST PRACTICE AND INTERVENTIONS IN CRISIS DISASTER, AND TRAUMA

PART III / OPERATIONALIZING GENERALIST SOCIAL WORK PRACTICE IN THE WAKE OF DISASTER: CASE STUDIES

Chapter 5: Micro Level Generalist Practice: Interventions with Individuals, Families, and Groups

PART IV / CONCLUSION

Preface

The purpose of this book is to provide social workers with a conceptual framework and practice skills to understand and respond to the tragic events of September 11 and other disasters as they impact on individuals, families, groups, organizations, and communities. We have written this book because we believe that social workers have made and will continue to make a unique contribution in response to these events, other disasters, and their far reaching reverberations. We have sought to make sense out of the potentially overwhelming and paralyzing effects of this and other disasters by offering a framework for active intervention based on the knowledge, values, and skills that social workers possess.

We have written this book from the multiple perspectives of social work educators and practitioners, as well as residents of New York City. As social work educators, we hope to contribute our expertise and perspectives to social work students and practitioners, as it is likely that September 11 and its consequences will have a defining impact on the future scope of social work practice. As social work practitioners and residents of New York City who, along with many others, provided services to victims and survivors of the World Trade Center attacks, we experienced the events in a very personal way. This combination of perspectives further compelled us to provide social workers with a framework, gleaned from our professional knowledge base, practice wisdom, and personal experience, to guide social work practice with all those affected by disaster.

Plan of the Book

Part I of this book provides an introduction to both the disaster of September 11 and generalist social work practice. Chapter 1 discusses the attacks on the World Trade Center in New York City and the Pentagon in Arlington, Virginia, as well as the plane crash in rural Pennsylvania, and the ways in which the far reaching reverberations of these events intersect with the history, mission, values, knowledge base, and skills of the social work profession. Chapter 2 presents an overview of the generalist approach to social work practice that provides an important conceptual framework and practice skills to guide social work intervention with individuals, families, groups, organizations, and communities.

In keeping with the adage, "theory without experience is mere intellectual play, and experience without theory is blind," this book includes both a theoretical section and a section containing multiple practice examples that are grounded in the theories presented. Part II provides the theoretical foundations for generalist practice and crisis intervention that can guide social work practice in the aftermath of disaster. Chapter 3 introduces several important theories and perspectives comprising the generalist social work knowledge base, including the systems approach, strengths and empowerment perspectives, and ego psychology. Chapter 4 presents theoretical foundations and practice principles that are specific to handling crisis, disaster and trauma.

Part III utilizes case studies of practice with individuals, families, groups, organizations, and communities that we provided, along with our students and colleagues, following the September 11 disaster to illustrate the ways in which the theoretical foundations outlined in Part II can be applied to generalist social work practice. To this end, Chapter 5 focuses on micro level generalist practice with individuals, families, and groups by presenting practice vignettes from a variety of social work settings, including counseling, family service, and school settings. Chapter 6 focuses on mezzo level generalist practice within agencies and organizations by presenting social work practice that was provided within a large child welfare agency in New York City. Chapter 7 illustrates macro level practice through discussion of the planning, coordination, and implementation of services within the larger New York City community following September 11.

In each chapter of Part III practice illustrations, in which names and places have been disguised for purposes of confidentiality, highlight critical aspects of generalist practice that are discussed throughout the book. These fundamental generalist practice principles include:

1) Starting where the client is

2) Working in the context of person in environment

3) The ways in which assessment of needs and subsequent interventions are shaped by setting and context

4) The different levels of intervention: micro, mezzo, and macro, regardless of what appears to be the presenting level for intervention

5) The multiple roles assumed by the generalist practitioner

In Chapters 5, 6, and 7, examples are presented and followed by a discussion section that underscores these central generalist practice principles that are further explicated throughout the book.

Finally, in Chapter 8 we review the lessons that have been learned from September 11 and its aftermath, and suggest future directions for social work practice, policy, education, and research in situations of disaster. Given our beginning understanding of September 11 and the reverberations of these events, this book is intended to provide an overview of generalist practice and crisis intervention and focuses on practice principles applicable to the first phase of intervention in a disaster. With an acknowledgement that we all have more to learn as the reverberations of these events unfold, at the end of Chapter 8 we have included a section entitled *Resources for Further Learning*. This bibliography of resources provides the reader with a starting point for continuing research and study regarding this important area of social work practice.

As we all learn from the tragic events of September 11, our hope is that this book will provide social work students and practitioners with some beginning guidance and structure for gathering, assimilating, conceptualizing, and operationalizing such knowledge in the service of all those impacted by these events and other forms of disaster.

Acknowledgements

We would like to acknowledge and thank many people who were instrumental in the process of researching and writing this book. Our colleagues at New York University Ehrenkranz School of Social Work offered much appreciated guidance and support. First, we would like to thank Associate Dean Jeane Anastas for her invaluable leadership and direction of the faculty and staff within the School of Social Work in its response to the events of September 11. Dr. Anastas organized the outstanding expertise of the faculty in a coordinated volunteer effort to meet the needs of individuals, families, groups, and organizations within the University and in the greater New York City community.

We would also like to thank Dean Suzanne England for her leadership and ongoing support. We are especially indebted to our colleague and mentor, Dr. Maryellen Noonan, who encouraged us to undertake this project, gave us feedback and guidance throughout, and was also instrumental in organizing the school's response to the child welfare practice community. We appreciate the ongoing support and guidance of colleagues at the School of Social Work, particularly Dr. Martha Gabriel, Dr. Gary Holden, Dr. Deborah Padgett, and Dr. Marge Rock.

We appreciate our students' contributions to this work, as they shared their experiences with individuals and families affected by September 11 and engaged in stimulating classroom discourse that helped us to further conceptualize and refine our ideas. We also wish to recognize the numerous practice settings represented in our vignettes that provided services for those affected by the events of September 11.

We are very grateful to Gabriella Amabile and Franchesca Dávila for their essential technical assistance in the preparation of this manuscript. Laura Brennan of Wadsworth Thomson Learning provided us with the opportunity to bring our ideas to a wider audience through the writing of this book. She has been consistently enthusiastic and supportive of our work.

Andrew Gelman and Mary Mirabito very generously read multiple drafts of the manuscript and provided thoughtful and helpful editorial feedback and assistance. We are very grateful for their heartfelt interest in and support of our work.

Diane Mirabito developed the original idea and conceptualization that became the foundation for this book. This conceptualization was enlarged upon and further developed by both authors, who drew upon their collective experience as professors of generalist social work practice at New York University's Ehrenkranz School of Social Work and as social work practitioners who volunteered within the University and New York City communities following September 11. As coauthors and colleagues, we have made equal contributions to writing this book and consider it a shared project. Throughout this endeavor we have been both challenged and enriched by our collaboration and we have learned immeasurably from our respective strengths and points of view. The result of our collaboration and exchange has been a richer and more complex work, which we hope will be a contribution to the social work response to September 11 and beyond.

Diane Mirabito

Caroline Rosenthal

About the Authors

Diane Mirabito, D.S.W., is an Assistant Professor at New York University Ehrenkranz School of Social Work, where she teaches courses in generalist practice, crisis and short term intervention, and clinical practice with adolescents. Her professional career includes extensive experience in clinical practice, supervision to social work staff and students, and program development in a variety of healthcare, school, and community based agency settings. Her research interests include risk and resilience among culturally diverse adolescents, adolescents' utilization of and termination from mental health services, and crisis and short term treatment approaches.

Dr. Mirabito received a B.A. from Syracuse University, a Masters in Social Work from the University of Chicago, School of Social Service Administration, and a Doctorate in Social Welfare from the Hunter College School of Social Work of the City University of New York. She maintains a private practice with adolescents and adults and is a consultant to social workers in community based organizations.

Caroline Rosenthal, Ph.D., is an Assistant Professor at New York University Ehrenkranz School of Social Work, where she teaches generalist practice, clinical practice with individuals and families, and a course on theories of human development. Her research includes studies of the needs of the Latino elderly, the use of psychodynamically informed treatment with Latinos, and the effectiveness of a manualized cognitive behavioral group treatment for depressed Latinas. She has also recently co produced a clinical social work training video entitled <u>Why Am I Here?: Engaging the Reluctant Client,</u> based on students' experiences in field placement.

Dr. Rosenthal currently serves as a member of the study group for the National Membership Committee on Psychoanalysis in Clinical Social Work and is co chair of the Committee on Ethnic and Cultural Diversity of the American Psychoanalytic Association. She graduated from Harvard College, received an M.S.W. from the University of California, Berkeley, a Ph.D. from Smith College School for Social Work, and has practiced in community mental health settings with diverse populations for over ten years.

About the Cover

"The World Trade Center, the crisis, the disaster, is in our faith and in our faces." Words similar to these, spoken in early October, inspired the cover created by Mollie Marr, an undergraduate at New York University. She describes her work in this way:

All of the squares in the collage are taken from images of September 11, 2001 and the events following. The irises are created from pictures of the towers and debris, because for so many days those were the only images that entered our vision. The white parts of the eyes are from smoke, because we had smoke in our eyes literally, and because our vision was clouded figuratively. The eyebrows of the central figure are also created from smoke, rendering them unable to serve their function, which is to protect the eye. The shading around the eyes and face are all taken from pictures of the towers, as the darkness and sleeplessness was caused by thoughts and images of them. All three faces come from pictures of everyone involved: President Bush, Osama Bin Laden, the terrorists, firefighters, police officers, health professionals, victims, Palestinians, New Yorkers, and Americans, arranged in a manner that attempts to create unity out of chaos and differences. The faces in profile reveal the workings of the mind, one is filled with debris, while the other is filled with smoke, one is looking inward, while the other is looking out, both are crying. The central figure is holding the other two in his/her arms while also holding a candle in one hand, an image from the memorials, but also an image of faith.

The light from the candle is the fire from the impact, and the darkness where the heart is comes from the holes left by the planes' impact. The body is composed of portions of pictures of the towers, and evokes prison imagery. One of the hands of the anguished face in profile is composed only of blood from various photos, representing the victims, the perpetrators' crime, and also our connection to blood as a commonality, our willingness to share it for the lives of others, and a reminder of common loss. Each person is dealing with the tragedy in a different manner, looking, asking, and grieving in his/her own way, his/her silent way. All are connected and held together even though they exist as individuals.

Mollie Marr

PART I

INTRODUCTION:
GENERALIST SOCIAL WORK PRACTICE
IN THE WAKE OF DISASTER

Chapter 1

The Impact of September 11 and Social Work's Response

Trauma is a catastrophic event outside the realm of normal human experience "that involves actual or threatened death or serious injury, or other threat to one's physical integrity; or witnessing an event that involves death, injury, or a threat to the physical integrity of another person; or learning about unexpected or violent death, serious harm, or threat of death or injury experienced by a family member or other close associate" (American Psychiatric Association, 2000, p. 463). By this definition, almost everyone in the United States experienced trauma as a result of the attacks on the World Trade Center in New York City and the Pentagon in Arlington, Virginia, and the airplane crash in rural Pennsylvania on September 11, 2001.

These events and their aftermath have created a situation with only a few precedents, such as the Oklahoma City bombing, to guide social work's response. Unlike natural disasters such as hurricanes, earthquakes, and tornados, these events were the consequence of intentional human acts, which makes them more incomprehensible and confusing. Assumptions about humanity, security, and justice were shattered, and a crisis of meaning was created for many. Why and how could someone do this? How could it have been prevented? Why wasn't it prevented? Indeed, studies show that rates of Post Traumatic Stress Disorder (PTSD), a reaction to trauma beyond the expectable response that leads to impairment in functioning and clinically significant distress, are greater and longer lasting following human caused events than for those arising from natural causes (Bell, 1995; Solomon & Green, 1992).

Furthermore, unlike many natural disasters and some man made ones, in which there are early indications of coming events, there was no warning or chance to prepare or escape the events of September 11. If people have foreknowledge of or prior experience with an event, however traumatic, they feel less frightened and powerless by having some opportunity to prepare (Norris & Murrell, 1988).

Unlike many traumatic events, which have a discrete beginning and end, this trauma is ongoing and without discernible conclusion. The violence and potential for further attacks did not end on September 11. Indeed, for months after, many people remained in a state of heightened anxiety, reacting to threats of further violence such as bridge bombings or acts of bioterrorism. Anthrax spores sent through the mail resulted in the death of five individuals and made bioterrorism a reality (Schwartz, 2001). Furthermore, the United States became involved in military action in Afghanistan, with the increased potential for loss of life. Without a clear end, the task is made more difficult for social workers to assess the magnitude and impact of the event and thus complicates identification of and response to potential need (Galea et al., 2002; Soliman, 2000).

The events of September 11 and their far reaching consequences have had and will continue to have a pervasive, all encompassing impact we are just starting to realize and understand. These events have affected all systems–individuals, families, organizations, communities, and the nation–to different degrees. This book will illustrate how social work's knowledge base and skills can be utilized to address these profound concerns.

Emotional and Psychological Consequences and Needs

Experience with previous disasters tells us that while there is a wide range of individual reactions to a catastrophic event, there are certain groups that are at greater risk for emotional and psychological consequences, depending on the degree of exposure to the disaster and previous psychosocial vulnerabilities (Ell & Aisenberg, 1998; Hoff, 2001; Parad & Parad, 1990; Solomon & Green, 1992; Tucker, Pfefferbaum, Nixon, & Foy, 1999; Wright, Ursano, Bartone, & Ingraham, 1990). One such high risk population is the thousands of survivors who escaped from the Pentagon, World Trade Center, and the surrounding areas. All were in danger of dying, many were physically injured, and many witnessed the death of others, including their friends and colleagues.

Research on survivors of the Oklahoma City bombing indicates nearly universal symptoms of intrusive reexperiencing of the event and hyperarousal (North et al., 1999). In addition, 45% of the survivors studied had post disaster psychiatric symptoms, and 34% met criteria for Post Traumatic Stress Disorder [described in Chapter 4] (North et al., 1999). Research on survivors of natural disasters also points to an increased prevalence of Post Traumatic Stress Disorder (PTSD) and depression, as well as an increase in suicide rates (Krug et al., 1998). All this research suggests that those who survived the attacks of September 11 are particularly vulnerable to emotional and psychological sequelae, and specific interventions must be tailored to meet their needs.

Thousands of people were displaced from homes and workplaces located in the stricken areas for weeks or even months following the attacks; the Red Cross paid housing expenses, including hotel fees, for about 8,500 refugees (Stewart, 2001). Many homes were destroyed or considered too dangerous to inhabit, requiring these families to find new housing. This subsequent displacement can cause or contribute to emotional and psychological problems.

A second very vulnerable population is the group that lost family, friends, and colleagues as a result of the events of September 11 (Green, Grace, & Gleser, 1985). Within this group of bereaved there will be populations with special needs, such as children who lost a parent (Belter, Dunn, & Jeney, 1991; Gammon, Daugherty, Finch, Belter, & Foster, 1993; Pynoos, 1992), parents who survive children (Margolis et al., 1988; Phifer, 1990), and domestic partners who may be disenfranchised grievers because their status may not be legally and socially recognized (Doka, 1989). Few of the families of the many undocumented immigrants who worked at the World Trade Center have sought counseling or other forms of assistance, fearing their legal status will be discovered (Kugel, 2001). Special outreach efforts may be necessary to serve them.

The loss of foreign nationals from over 100 countries underscores the diversity across ethnicity, race, culture, socioeconomic status, religion, and national origin of the people likely to need assistance in the wake of this disaster, and highlights the importance of providing culturally sensitive services to these populations, a hallmark of the social work profession (NASW, 1999). Examples of outreach services and work with some of these vulnerable populations will be presented in Chapter 5.

Rescue workers constitute another population potentially vulnerable to serious emotional and psychological reactions (Armstrong, Lund, Townsend McWright, & Tichenor, 1995). Police officers and firefighters experienced or witnessed the devastation at very close range, for prolonged periods of time, and were physically injured at the site (Lipton & Johnson, 2001). Hundreds of their colleagues were killed. As a result, rescue and recovery workers and all those involved in the clean up of the site are also at risk for emotional consequences.

There is also the unique psychological impact of this catastrophic event on populations who were already experiencing severe psychosocial stressors or emotional disorders before September 11 (Earls et al., 1988; Nolen Hoeksema & Morrow, 1991; Soliman & Rogge, 2002). For example, children in foster care may exhibit significant behavioral and emotional symptoms because of their existing vulnerability to issues of loss and lack of safety and security. The impact on vulnerable populations can manifest in unexpected ways. There were reports that many shelters for victims of domestic violence experienced a drop in the number of women seeking services. Among the explanations was that in the aftermath people wanted to feel connected and a sense of belonging, so women were more reluctant to leave abusive situations, and abusers used the attacks to coerce them by stating that now, more than ever, family was important (Lewin, 2001).

A significant number of people without direct connection to victims or the sites also experienced strong physical, mental, emotional and behavioral reactions, which are normal and expectable, given the devastating nature of the attacks and the constant exposure through the media. Education, clarification, and reassurance regarding such reactions are necessary to reduce anxiety and to assess those who may require professional assistance. Children are particularly vulnerable to these strong reactions, and parents and teachers can be taught techniques to help allay fears and recognize those children who need additional intervention

(Green et al., 1991). Examples of these situations will be illustrated in Chapters 5 and 6.

Research indicates that there are differential reactions to disaster based on gender and age. For example, girls and women appear to have greater levels of symptomatology and diagnosable PTSD than males (Burke et al., 1986; Green et al., 1991; Steinglass & Gerrity, 1990). Despite common misconceptions about their fragility, older adults tend to cope well with disaster (Huerta & Horton, 1978; Kilijanek & Drabek, 1979). Further research that explores differential response to disaster will be necessary, and social workers will in turn have to tailor their interventions to meet the needs of specific populations.

In recognition of the immense emotional and psychological toll of the events of September 11, $28 million in federal funds were awarded for mental health and substance abuse counseling (Blair, 2001). The need for these types of interventions was highlighted by statistics indicating that prescriptions for anti anxiety and anti depressant medication increased dramatically following the attacks. For example, in Washington, D. C. prescriptions for these medications increased by 13 percent (Blair, 2001). In Manhattan, visits to mental health clinics increased by 50 percent (Blair, 2001).

The first study of PTSD and depression in Manhattan residents following the attacks of September 11 underscores the dramatic emotional and psychological consequences of these acts. Of the over 1,000 adults interviewed, 7.5% met criteria for PTSD and 9.7 % met criteria for depression. This is approximately twice the baseline rate for these disorders. Consistent with previous research cited in this chapter, proximity to the site, degree of exposure (for example death of a friend or relative or loss of a job), low level of social support, panic attack during or shortly after the events, and two or more prior stressors were all predictors of PTSD. Interestingly and with significant implications for social workers, who are committed to culturally sensitive practice, Hispanic ethnicity was also a positive predictor of PTSD and depression (Galea et al., 2002).

Given their training and skills, social workers are well equipped to address and help ameliorate the emotional and psychological consequences of trauma. As will be illustrated in Part III of this book, they can do so through direct individual, group, and family interventions, as well as through psychoeducational and preventive efforts addressing the specific needs of each of these populations differentially impacted by disaster.

Economic Consequences and Needs

There are also dramatic economic consequences of September 11 at individual, community, state, national, and even global levels. The attack "brought the economy of the United States to a temporary standstill and continue[s] to affect people's confidence, and willingness to spend money, even in Europe" (Leonhardt, 2001, p. WK 3).

It is estimated that New York City will eventually lose about 100,000 jobs because of the ripple effects of the terrorist attacks (McKinley, 2001b). For example, fear of flying among passengers and increased costs of security for airlines led to massive layoffs of airline employees (Sharkey, 2001). Queens, a borough of New York City and the site of two airports, was especially hard hit. More than 41,000 people work for airlines or the airports, and between 5,000 and 8,000 jobs may be lost to cutbacks (Kershaw, 2001). In addition, there are 20,000 jobs in businesses related to air travel, such as travel agencies and parking lots. For every 1,000 air transport jobs lost, it is estimated that 470 positions in these related industries will be lost as well.

In New York State, weekly unemployment claims have more than doubled following September 11 (McKinley, 2001b). Unemployment means loss of income, benefits, social status, and identity to individuals and their families. These tremendous economic, social, and psychological costs can be addressed by social workers in a variety of ways, such as referrals for vocational training, securement of unemployment benefits, and provision of supportive case management and counseling services.

The New York City Comptroller's office released a report estimating that the local economic cost of the attack will be $90 to $105 billion over the next three years (Blair, 2001). The cost of rescue, recovery, and rebuilding operations has been and will continue to be enormous; some have estimated it will reach $35 billion (Kahn, 2001). The loss of jobs and workplaces has directly affected the city and state's tax revenues. These economic pressures resulting from the attacks have contributed in large measure to a $1 billion budget shortfall in New York City for the year 2001, and an estimated budget deficit of $4 billion for the following year (Berenson, 2001; Steinhauer, 2001).

The budget shortfall, in turn, will affect almost every city agency, including recreational, social, and health services. Almost all agencies have been asked to cut their budgets by 15% (Steinhauer, 2001). Such cuts, of course, will directly affect the availability and quality of important services to thousands of clients, especially the most vulnerable populations that social workers are likely to serve. For example, a new H.I.V. prevention campaign and a program designed to combat high infant mortality rates in some areas of the city may no longer be funded (Steinhauer, 2001).

The fiscal crisis also meant a delay of and reduction in the amount of money available to the State Legislature for disbursement to charities, further affecting benefits and services to needy populations. A social service program focused on serving Haitian women had to lay off a social worker who helped people dying of AIDS make arrangements for the caretaking of their children (McKinley, 2001a). A legal services center representing the poor laid off 21 lawyers and paralegals (McKinley, 2001a).

In addition, because of the enormous outpouring of financial support for organizations raising money for victims of September 11, private gifts to traditional charities declined (Donovan, 2001). Thus, at a time when the number of people requesting or requiring assistance has increased as a result of the economic downturn, charities have even more limited resources to offer these poor and otherwise vulnerable populations traditionally served by social workers. In these less direct ways, the attacks of September 11 have affected thousands of people.

Vast amounts of money were raised by multiple organizations for those impacted by the disaster, leading to questions about the nature of its disbursement. For example, funds raised specifically for rescue workers who died on September 11 (at least $353 million as of December 2001), has led families of civilian victims to feel that there is an "aristocracy of grief" (Barstow & Henriques, 2001, p. B7), with rescue workers' lives being more highly valued. As part of their jobs, social workers are frequently in the position of making decisions regarding the distribution of limited resources. Thus, social workers have special expertise in dealing with the question of how to do so in an equitable and just manner. This expertise could be fruitfully brought to bear on this delicate situation of victim compensation.

Consequences for Civil Liberties and Social Justice

In response to the events of September 11, new laws and revised federal regulations designed to increase security have given the government greater power to detain, investigate and prosecute suspects. For example, the President has authorized the use of secret military tribunals for non citizens accused of terrorism and the monitoring of conversations between some prisoners and their lawyers (Toner, 2001). Federal investigators contacted administrators on more than 200 college campuses searching for information regarding students from Middle Eastern countries (Purdy, 2001). Approximately 5,000 young Middle Eastern men in the United States on temporary visas were interviewed by these authorities. In addition, about 500 people, many nationals of Middle Eastern countries, were detained for violating immigration laws; most of these violations would not have resulted in detention prior to September 11 (Wilgoren, 2001).

These actions raise concerns about the potential infringement of civil liberties, especially for foreign nationals living in the United States, since suspects may be singled out on the basis of nationality or ethnicity (Purdy, 2001; Rosen, 2001; Wilgoren, 2001). Arab American groups have reported that people of Arab descent feel they are experiencing discrimination in the community and workplace because of their nationality or religion (Matloff, 2001; Toner, 2001). Although it is unclear whether discrimination actually has occurred, about 100 individuals have filed complaints with the Federal Equal Employment Opportunity Commission (Belluk, 2001). Such incidents are cause for concern to social work, a profession deeply committed to social justice. Moreover, they underscore the need for social workers to advocate for and empower such potentially vulnerable groups.

Consequences for Social Policy and Social Service Delivery

As is evident from the consequences and needs described above, victims of the attacks, whether those directly and immediately harmed or those impacted as a result of the reverberations of this event, all may be in need of a great deal of services and concrete resources, such as mental health and medical treatment, employment and housing services, and financial and health care entitlements. Social workers play crucial roles in the development and provision of services as case managers, advocates, program planners, and policy developers. As discussed in Chapter 7, at the Family Assistance Center in New York, established to aid the World Trade Center victims and their families, legal, medical, financial, mental health, and residential services were available in one location with requests processed in a very expedient manner. Such innovations warrant review as possible templates for the way services and benefits should be generally provided to those requiring assistance.

In another example, while before the attack one in four New York City residents had no health insurance, the layoffs precipitated by this event made this number far greater (Finkelstein, 2001). In response, the state offered four months of disaster relief Medicaid to all low income residents of the city, not just those directly affected by the attacks. In a six week period, 75,000 families applied. Prior to September 11, about 8,000 individuals had applied for Medicaid each month (Finkelstein, 2001). The paperwork and enrollment criteria were greatly simplified, and approval was almost immediate, rather than the typical 90 day wait, making health care truly accessible. Such a model of universal, streamlined access to benefits should be considered for its potential replication to other programs relevant to the populations social workers have historically served. The impact of the attacks on social policy and delivery of social services will be further discussed in Chapters 7 and 8.

Consequences for Social Work Research

Stress and human response to it has been examined rigorously and extensively, particularly in the latter half of the 20th century (Ell & Aisenberg, 1998). However, given the virtually unprecedented nature of the attacks of September 11, there is limited information on the type and level of reactions and consequences that can be expected as a result of these events at an individual, family, group, organizational, community, and national level, and how these can best be addressed. What aspects of our current knowledge base are relevant to these unique circumstances? What are the long term consequences of these events? Will there be differential responses and will they require specialized interventive approaches? What sorts of interventions, programs, and policies will prove to be useful? How can these be evaluated? Social workers have an ethical responsibility to contribute to the knowledge base of the profession (NASW, 1999), and with its person in environment approach, further described in Chapter 2, social work has a unique perspective through which to pose, examine, and answer such questions.

Hope and Resilience

In an effort to show the important role social work can play in response to disaster, this chapter illustrated some of the detrimental consequences of September 11 from the perspective of how these intersect with the mission, values, skills, and knowledge base of the social work profession. Chapter 3 will discuss another cornerstone of social work practice, the strengths perspective, which highlights the capacities, resilience, coping, and adaptation of human beings. Thus, it is also critical to focus on the glimmers of hope and strength amidst such seemingly vast devastation and despair. People have been bolstered by the courage and altruism of the rescue workers and civilians who risked their lives, and by the generosity of people who have given money, time, and of themselves to help those impacted by this tragedy (Crossette, 2001; Jacobs, 2001). In an example of communal caretaking, a town that lost 36 of its residents in the attacks has collected money and asked local businesses to donate goods and services, such as plumbing and lawn care, to the affected families (Jacobs, 2001).

The September 11 attacks have also been instrumental in accelerating the peace process in Northern Ireland (Lyall, 2001). In the new climate, fearful of being labeled terrorists, the Irish Republican Army agreed to decommission their arsenal, reviving the stalled peace process (Lyall, 2001).

The tragedy of September 11 may also produce blueprints for more efficient, dignified, equitable service provision to the populations traditionally served by social workers, and may spur our profession to develop new models of practice which focus on prevention, early intervention, and community based services (Soliman, 1996; Soliman & Poulin, 1997; Soliman, Raymond, & Lingle, 1996).

Summary

The wide range of consequences outlined in this chapter are just a few examples of the pervasive, all encompassing impact of the September 11 attacks and how they interface with the mission, values, knowledge base, and skills of the social work profession. Currently, and in many ways we have yet to realize, the attacks of September 11 and their reverberations will clearly constitute one of the major events defining the problems the next generation of social workers will be called upon to address.

Employing a generalist approach to practice, described in Chapter 2, social workers view each situation in context and intervene at all different system levels affected using a wide repertoire of roles and skills. This perspective offers a way of conceptualizing the exceedingly complex situation arising out of the events of September 11, and shaping a social work response at all levels of need. This is the conceptual framework and approach that will be presented in this book and which has guided the social work interventions described herein.

Chapter 2

Generalist Social Work Practice:
An Overview

A Rationale for Generalist Practice

As discussed in Chapter 1, the events of September 11 affected everyone in metropolitan New York City, the United States, and around the world on multiple levels and in varied ways. The wide ranging emotional, economic, familial, interpersonal, psychological, political, and social effects of this event have been and will continue to be felt by individuals, families, organizations, institutions, communities, and the nation at large. The pervasive and complex impact of the disaster calls for a broad based social work practice approach that is able to address a wide range of needs. Generalist practice offers social work practitioners such an approach by providing a conceptual framework and a set of skills to intervene at multiple levels and in diverse ways.

Generalist practice has been defined as "the application of an eclectic knowledge base, professional values, and a wide range of skills to target any size system for change" (Kirst Ashman & Hull, 1999, p. 5). As defined by these authors, generalist practice enables practitioners to provide a diverse array of interventions to systems that range in size from individuals, families, and groups to organizations, institutions, communities, and the larger society. Specifically, the generalist approach enables practitioners to intervene at any and all of these levels with many different kinds of services, including prevention, education, counseling, the provision of concrete resources, advocacy, organizational change and development, community development, and political action. In order for social workers to effectively respond to the all encompassing effects of the September 11 disaster, they must utilize this diverse range of skills and interventions.

This chapter provides an overview of generalist social work practice by describing five elements central to this approach that will be further discussed and illustrated throughout this book. These five elements also provide a useful framework for intervention in situations of disaster. These elements include:

1) The *person in environment perspective* as the theoretical underpinning of generalist practice

2) The multiple levels of generalist intervention: *micro, mezzo*, and *macro* levels

3) The diverse *roles* of generalist practitioners

4) The integration of *direct practice, policy*, and *research*

5) The five stages of generalist practice:
   Engagement, assessment, and the *planning, implementation,* and *evaluation* of *interventions*

The Person in Environment Perspective

In order to address the wide range of problems that resulted from the September 11 disaster and to intervene within systems of all sizes, generalist practitioners must acquire and utilize an eclectic knowledge base. The primary theoretical conceptualization underlying this knowledge base is the person in environment perspective, which is concerned with understanding the interrelationships between people and their environments. This conceptualization is referred to as an "ecological" framework (Zastrow, 2000, p. 70), and focuses on the interactions of individuals with many environmental systems, such as the family, educational, political, religious, and social service systems. Generalist social work practitioners help individuals, families, groups, organizations, and communities work toward change in any and all of these systems.

Generalist practice utilizes an eclectic knowledge base that draws from a variety of psychological, environmental, and organizational approaches and theories, such as ego psychology, systems, ecosystems, and empowerment approaches, as well as a strengths perspective. The generalist practice model utilizes key aspects of these various approaches, perspectives, and theories to understand and explain the relationships and linkages between individuals and the multiple environmental systems with which they interact, such as the family, workplace, community, institutions, and the larger society. Chapter 3, The Knowledge Base for Generalist Practice, further describes each of these approaches and theories and identifies the unique aspects that each contributes to the knowledge base of generalist practice.

In addition to this diverse and eclectic knowledge base, the generalist practitioner is guided by core values integral to the social work profession. These core values include regard and respect for an individual's worth, dignity, integrity, and competence; for the unique characteristics of diverse populations; and for the individual's right to make independent decisions and to participate actively in the helping process. The core values of the social work profession also include a commitment to assist client systems obtain needed resources; make social institutions more humane and responsive to human needs; and foster social justice (NASW, 1999).

Multiple Levels of Intervention: Micro, Mezzo, and Macro

A unique and distinguishing aspect of generalist practice is its commitment to prepare practitioners to assess needs and plan interventions at all levels of client systems. By taking a broad perspective of people within their environments, the generalist practitioner is prepared to view problems holistically and plan interventions that address all the systems that contribute to problem situations.

By conducting a thorough assessment of needs within the entire client system, the generalist practitioner identifies problems that require resolution and determines at which level or levels of intervention change efforts should be planned and implemented. Thus, rather than being constrained by a particular method or modality of intervention, such as individual or group therapy, the generalist practitioner chooses the type and location of interventions based on a careful assessment of needs. This process allows the practitioner to think broadly, flexibly, and creatively about practice.

The generalist model of practice delineates three levels of intervention, which correspond to client systems of different sizes. Micro level interventions are those that address change with individuals, families, and groups. Mezzo level interventions are aimed at change within institutions, agencies, and organizations. Macro level interventions target change within broader systems, such as communities and the larger society. The following descriptions of micro, mezzo, and macro interventions include examples of generalist social work practice at each level in response to the September 11 disaster.

Micro Level Practice

Social work intervention at the micro level is defined as direct practice with individuals, couples, families, and groups. At this level of practice, social workers provide direct services to clients in face to face contacts as well as by negotiating with systems to obtain and coordinate services on behalf of clients. In micro level practice, the generalist practitioner focuses change efforts in multiple areas, including: the psychological, emotional, and personal functioning of individuals; interpersonal functioning between individuals, families, or groups, and problematic conditions within the social environment (Hepworth, Rooney, & Larsen, 2002; Miley, O'Melia, & DuBois, 2001).

In response to the September 11 disaster, generalist social work practitioners utilized micro level skills to assist individuals, families, and groups with concrete, psychological, and emotional concerns. Examples of micro level practice in response to the disaster included:

- Assessment, crisis intervention, short term counseling, and the provision of referrals for concrete resources and longer term counseling at urban and suburban counseling, family service, and community mental health settings as well as at a Family Assistance Center which was set up to serve individuals and families who were coping with the tragedy of missing and lost loved ones

- Crisis intervention, support, and bereavement counseling for families at the morgue where the deceased were identified

- Crisis services for rescue workers and for the family members of lost rescue workers at employee assistance programs

- Ongoing crisis intervention services for individuals and families of those who witnessed and survived the disaster

Chapter 5 presents case examples of practice with individuals, families, and groups, which will illustrate and further explicate interventions utilized in micro level practice.

Mezzo Level Practice

Mezzo level practice focuses on organizational change within social service agencies and other organizations that provide social work services, such as schools and hospitals (Miley et al., 2001). Interventions at this level are targeted to change the internal structure and functioning of systems that affect clients in order to either directly or indirectly improve services to them (Hepworth et al., 2002). Mezzo level organizational change efforts can include consultation and interdisciplinary collaboration with professionals from varied disciplines, such as medical teams in hospitals or educational staff in school settings.

Examples of mezzo level practice in response to the disaster included:

- Consultation, education, and training regarding normal and expectable reactions to trauma within all kinds of organizations, ranging from schools to occupational, social service, and healthcare settings

- Psychoeducational parents' groups to assist parents in helping their children better cope with the disaster

- Consultation and training forums to help teachers and principals at elementary, middle, and secondary schools address, support, and cope with students' expectable reactions to the disaster

- Training for doctors, nurses, and ancillary staff in healthcare settings to help them recognize signs and symptoms of trauma in patients who might be presenting with physical complaints

- Institutionalized "debriefing" groups for rescue workers and for anyone who experienced or witnessed the disaster

Chapter 6 presents examples of mezzo level generalist interventions, which are directed at working with groups toward organizational development and organizational change, undertaken in response to September 11.

Macro Level Practice

In contrast to direct practice interventions with individuals, families, groups, and organizations, generalist practice at the macro level includes indirect interventions, such as planning, coordinating, and implementing social services as well as analyzing and formulating policies in response to social problems. Macro level practitioners assist client systems at community, city, state, and federal levels to organize, plan, develop, administer, deliver, and evaluate services (Hepworth et al., 2002). Generalist practice at the macro level also includes community organization and development, and social and political action.

Examples of macro level practice in response to the September 11 disaster included:

- The organization of funds for special and affected populations, such as bereaved families and undocumented family members of the deceased

- The promotion of just policies to protect discriminated and disenfranchised groups, such as gay partners and undocumented family members of the deceased

- Advocacy for the equitable distribution of benefits

- City wide interagency planning, organization, coordination, and implementation of crisis intervention, counseling, and concrete resources and services for thousands of survivors, their family members, bereaved families, and the general population

Chapter 7 will present several macro level practice examples of the ways that services were planned and delivered in New York City following the disaster.

Diverse Roles of Generalist Practitioners

In order to intervene at micro, mezzo, and macro levels with systems of any size, generalist practitioners must possess a broad range of skills and be equipped to assume a wide array of roles. Generalist social workers utilize these multiple roles interchangeably across all three levels of practice, depending on the system or systems that are targeted for change.

The following descriptions of roles assumed by generalist practitioners, adapted from Miley et al. (2001) and Hepworth et al. (2002), reflect the diverse and varied ways in which social workers intervene both directly with individuals, families, and groups, in organizations and communities, as well as within and between these systems.

Direct Service Provider: Several terms are used interchangeably to describe the direct services provided by social workers, including counseling, therapy, and psychotherapy.   In this role, a social worker can be referred to as a "counselor," "therapist," or "clinical social worker."   Direct services include: individual casework; couple, marital, and/or family counseling (psychotherapy); and group work services, including support, therapy, self help, task, and skill development groups (Hepworth et al., 2002).   The direct services described in this book were provided in a wide range of agency based and organizational settings.

Educator/Teacher: Generalist practitioners learn from their clients as well as provide information to help empower client systems (e.g. individuals, families, groups, organizations, communities) to resolve current difficulties and to prevent future ones.

Educator/Trainer: Generalist practitioners serve as educational resource specialists by making presentations, conducting workshops, or participating on educational panels.   Within organizations, generalist practitioners assess the needs of client or staff groups, develop goals, implement training strategies, and evaluate training programs.

Case Manager: Generalist practitioners assess clients' emotional, psychological, and environmental needs, and arrange, coordinate, and oversee the provision of counseling and concrete services. A case manager interacts directly with both clients and service providers (agencies or organizations) on the clients' behalf, to ensure that needed services are appropriately planned and delivered.

Consultant: Generalist practitioners are consultants both to other social workers and to a wide range of professionals who seek their unique expertise. As consultants to other social workers, they provide supervision and direction regarding practice and program development. As consultants to other service providers such as doctors, nurses, teachers, lawyers, and probation officers, generalist social workers help these professionals understand and intervene with clients in complex situations.

Interdisciplinary Collaborator: Related to the consultant role, generalist practitioners assess, plan, and collaborate as members of interdisciplinary teams with a wide range of professionals, such as psychiatrists, psychologists, speech or occupational therapists, teachers, and nurses, to provide comprehensive services to clients.

Facilitator: Social workers are often called upon to facilitate access to and provision of services to clients in a variety of ways. These include: connecting client systems to resources; fostering organizational development by activating the participation of organizational members in change efforts; enhancing linkages within organizations, helping organizations function more productively; and facilitating group processes.

Program Developer: In this role, the generalist practitioner assesses unmet needs of client groups and plans, develops, and implements new programs.

Planner: In the role of planner, the social worker coordinates program and policy development, conducts needs assessments within communities in order to understand social problems, and works with community leaders to develop solutions to problems.

Broker: Similar to the role of facilitator, as a broker, the social worker links and connects clients to available resources by providing information and making referrals.

Advocate: In the capacity of advocate, social workers function as intermediaries between clients and other systems to help obtain resources. In addition, as advocates, social workers facilitate fair and just treatment to client systems and develop social policies that foster equitable resource distribution.

Convener/Mediator: As a convener/mediator, social workers provide interagency linkage by coordinating, planning, mobilizing, and networking; bringing together community task groups and interagency committees; negotiating differences and resolving conflicts; identifying gaps in service delivery systems; and engaging in interagency planning.

Social Activist/Catalyst: As a social activist, the generalist practitioner identifies social problems and/or injustices; mobilizes resources; builds coalitions; engages in lobbying to change or create new legislation; and initiates and sustains social action.

Researcher: Generalist practitioners continuously critically examine and evaluate their interventions with individuals, families, groups, organizations, and communities in order to modify and further improve their practice. Moreover, they investigate a broad range of conditions affecting clients in order to contribute new knowledge for the profession.

The generalist practitioner assumes these multiple roles with a wide range of client systems, including individuals, families, groups, organizations, and communities, and intervenes at micro, mezzo, and macro levels of practice.

Integration of Direct Practice, Policy, and Research

As is evident in the descriptions of these diverse roles, generalist practice addresses all three primary areas of professional social work practice—direct practice, policy, and research—as well as the connections between these. Direct practice activities include those in which generalist practitioners work with individuals, couples, families, and groups to provide both counseling/therapeutic services and also to obtain and coordinate concrete resources and services.

Policy activities include the ways in which generalist practitioners develop, plan, implement, and evaluate the social welfare policies which determine how society distributes resources among members and directs the delivery of health and human services (Miley et al., 2001).

Research includes activities in which generalist practitioners systematically investigate a wide range of conditions—physical, environmental, cultural, psychological, and emotional—that impact client systems. Research also includes the evaluation of practice and the skills and capacity to be a critical consumer of research findings (Miley et al., 2001).

The Five Stages of Generalist Practice: Engagement, Assessment, and the Planning, Implementation, and Evaluation of Interventions

At all three levels of intervention, micro, mezzo, and macro, generalist practitioners engage in a change process that involves five stages. These five stages are: engagement, assessment, and the planning, implementation, and evaluation of interventions. The generalist change process utilizes a common set of skills that can be applied differentially to work with systems of any size. Hepworth et al. (2002) describe these five stages in the following ways:

Engagement

This first stage of generalist practice includes establishing rapport, developing trust, exploring the reason(s) for service and the view(s) of the problem from all relevant persons within the client system, assessing and enhancing motivation for change, and conveying the generalist practitioner's role in work with the client system.

Assessment

While simultaneously engaging the client system, the generalist practitioner conducts a biopsychosocial assessment by gathering pertinent information about the physical, emotional, psychological, familial, social, cultural and environmental spheres relevant to the presenting needs, problem(s), or situation. This biopsychosocial assessment includes multiple dimensions of the problem, and identifies both the various systems that contribute to the problem as well as the strengths, resources, and capabilities within the client system that can be utilized to solve the problem.

26

Planning Interventions

After conducting a thorough assessment, the generalist practitioner is able to collaboratively decide and plan, with the client system, what needs to be changed and what actions need to be taken to improve the problem situation. When the social worker and client arrive at consensus about the intervention plan, they collaboratively develop a contract that consists of a formal agreement specifying the goals and objectives to be accomplished, the strategies that will be implemented to accomplish the goals, and the roles and responsibilities of the social worker and client.

Implementation of Interventions

During this phase, the generalist practitioner works with the client system to implement a series of tasks designed to accomplish desired goals. The interventions that are implemented in this phase include those targeted at change within the individual, family, group, organization, and community, and within and between systems in the larger environment.

Evaluation of Interventions

The generalist practitioner monitors progress made toward agreed upon goals by engaging the client system in an ongoing dialogue about the change process. This assessment of progress is accomplished by utilizing subjective opinions from client systems as well as formalized instruments that measure and evaluate progress made toward targeted goals.

Summary

To summarize, the generalist practitioner:

- Utilizes the person in environment perspective

- Attends to the interaction within and between systems

- Intervenes at multiple levels, including micro level interventions with individuals, families, and groups; mezzo level interventions within institutions and organizations; and macro level interventions within communities and the larger society

- Assumes multiple roles, such as direct service provider, consultant, broker, interdisciplinary collaborator, program developer, educator, trainer, and community planner

- Has a wide repertoire of skills, which allow for engagement, assessment, planning, implementation, and evaluation of interventions

The following chapters offer an overview of the perspectives, approaches, and theories that make up the knowledge base of generalist practice and crisis intervention. In Part III we provide case examples that illustrate the application of generalist practice and crisis intervention in response to the events of September 11.

PART II

THEORETICAL FOUNDATIONS: GENERALIST PRACTICE AND INTERVENTIONS IN CRISIS, DISASTER, AND TRAUMA

Chapter 3

A Knowledge Base for Generalist Practice

The Knowledge Base of a Generalist Perspective

As detailed in the previous chapter, the hallmarks of a generalist social work perspective include grounding in a theoretical knowledge base that posits a focus on a person in environment perspective, intervention at micro, mezzo, and macro levels, and the assumption of multiple roles (Kirst Ashman & Hull, 1999; Miley et al., 2001; Poulin, 2000). In keeping with this broad base of conceptualization and intervention, the knowledge base for generalist practice draws from multiple theories and perspectives, but there is no one specific set of theories that comprise it. Given the fundamental generalist premises of assessment and intervention with both the individual and the environment, intervention at various levels and in multiple roles, and the strong value base of the profession, it is not surprising that a systems approach, as well as strengths and empowerment perspectives, are commonly cited as part of the knowledge base of generalist social work practice (Kirst Ashman & Hull, 1999; Miley et al., 2001; Poulin, 2000).

Following Sheafor, Horejsi, and Horejsi (2000), the multiple theories, models, and approaches used by social workers can be thought of as conceptual frameworks, "composed of a coherent set of concepts, beliefs, values, propositions, assumptions, hypotheses, and principles…that help one to understand people, how people function, and how people change" (p. 49). A conceptual framework is fundamental in helping the social worker organize the often overwhelming amount of information elicited in assessing client systems, and in guiding the techniques that are employed in the intervention (Ragg, 2001).

Subsumed under conceptual frameworks are orienting theories and practice frameworks. Orienting theories aim to describe and explain behaviors and problems and their etiology; practice frameworks offer ways of addressing such problems. Practice frameworks can be perspectives, models, or theories. A theory "offers both an explanation of certain behaviors or situations and guidance on how they can be changed" (Sheafor et al., 2000, p. 51). Perspectives, models and approaches are more descriptive and general and offer guidance regarding intervention. This chapter describes systems, strengths and empowerment perspectives, and ego psychological theory as different ways of organizing, analyzing, and intervening with client systems.

These four approaches provide a conceptual underpinning for the tenets of generalist practice discussed in the previous chapter, and fit exceedingly well with the history, mission, and values of the social work profession. Systems, strengths, and empowerment perspectives lead the social work practitioner to assess client systems in the context of their environments, focusing on strengths, rather than vulnerabilities. Ego psychology provides a framework for assessing an individual's strengths, coping and adaptation. These frameworks also target interventions at the micro, mezzo, and macro levels, if warranted, with a view toward empowering the client system as much as possible.

Any theory or perspective is a social construct and is inevitably tied to the socio cultural and historical context in which it was created. Consequently, any theory or approach must be critically examined for its utility with a particular client and situation, for the empirical data supporting its use, and for its congruency with the value base of the social work profession. Finally, these approaches and those specific to crisis, disaster, and trauma presented in the next chapter are but a few of the multiple and wide ranging theories, models and perspectives available to social workers.

A Systems Perspective

A system is defined as "a dynamic order of parts and processes standing in mutual interaction" (Bertalanffy, 1968, p. 208). The systems perspective, as employed in social work, describes "the principles by which systems function, grow, develop, and interact with other systems.

These principles are used to predict the behavior of biological and social systems and to formulate strategies for changing a system" (Sheafor et al., 2000, p. 89).

In terms of assessment, a systems approach views a person in the context of his or her environment, as well as the ongoing transactions that exist between them. Humans are seen as complex wholes with biological, psychological, social, cultural and spiritual components that at the same time are parts of larger systems, such as families, neighborhoods, groups, and communities. Since all parts of any system are interrelated and interconnected, the focus of attention is always on the interaction and fit between the individual and the other systems with which he or she interfaces.

Given this understanding, the planning and implementation of interventions includes changes both in the individual as well as the systems with which they interact. The systems perspective is congruent with the generalist approach described in Chapter 2, which focuses on the person in environment and the interaction between systems, and thus posits intervention at several levels and in one or more systems.

There are several key concepts in a systems approach that are helpful in assessment and planning of interventions. All systems are composed of smaller systems or subsystems and in turn are part of larger systems. Systems have a variety of dimensions such as structure, interaction, biopsychosocial dimensions, and cultural elements (Miley et al., 2001).

Structure refers to the arrangement of individuals and subsystems within a system. This arrangement can be described in terms of the boundaries delineating the system from its environment or the subsystems within systems. Boundaries can be open, allowing transactions between systems, or closed, limiting access and exchange of resources. Hierarchy, or identification of who has power, status, and privilege, is another way of describing a system's structure and, like an exploration of boundaries, can provide information as to why a subcomponent of the system may be experiencing problems and how these might be addressed.

Systems interact reciprocally with other systems and with the social and physical environment in ways that tend to maintain their equilibrium or status quo. This is one reason why it can be difficult to implement change. However, systems do evolve in response to internal and external forces. Thus, identifying, reinforcing, or modifying various patterns of behavior or interaction is one way a social worker can intervene to change a system.

Since all systems are interconnected, change in one part of the system creates change in all others. Thus, the system will change in response to its environment, and the environment in turn will respond to changes in the system. This provides a conceptual foundation for social work intervention at micro, mezzo, and macro levels, as relevant. Furthermore, the interconnection of systems means that often problems reside not in the individual, but in the goodness of fit with the environment, and that both environments and individuals can and should be the focus of change.

Just as systems have multiple components, the individual as a subsystem is seen as multidimensional, having biological, psychological, social, cultural, and spiritual aspects which interact with each other and the individual's context and environment to determine the individual's level of functioning, well being, adaptation and coping. Thus, at the individual level, a systems approach also provides a holistic and comprehensive way of looking at the person in environment, assessing needs, and fashioning appropriate interventions which target not just the individual, but multiple other systems with which they interact.

The Empowerment Approach

An empowerment approach in social work practice is both a "clinical and community oriented approach encompassing holistic work with individuals, families, small groups, communities, and political systems" (Lee, 2000b, p. 30 31). It focuses on identifying groups of people who have heretofore not had a voice in the decisions affecting their lives, and on facilitating their assumption of power, control, and influence (Lee, 2000a; Rappaport, 1990). Such disenfranchised groups are the very populations that social workers historically have been committed to serving. Thus this approach is consonant with the core values of social justice, dignity, and worth of the individual held by the social work profession.

Empowerment has been defined as:

> A process whereby the social worker engages in a set of activities with the client…that aim to reduce the powerlessness that has been created by negative valuations based on membership in a stigmatized group. It involves identification of the power blocks that contribute to the problem as well as the development and implementation of specific strategies aimed at either the reduction of the effects from indirect power blocks or the reduction of the operations of direct power blocks. (Solomon, 1976, p. 19)

Empowerment is a concept with personal, interpersonal, and political dimensions, making explicit connections between social and economic justice and personal travails (Lee, 2000a; Miley et al., 2001). An empowerment approach consists of seven foci, which serve as guidelines for areas explored in an assessment (Lee, 2000b):

1. A historical understanding of oppression

2. An ecological or systemic view of individuals, including their coping and adaptation to an often inequitable environment

3. An "ethclass perspective," the term used by Lee (2000a, p. 220) to describe an approach that understands ethnicity, race, and class as being interrelated, and focuses on the impact of racism and classism on individuals

4. A cultural and multicultural perspective that appreciates the impact of diversity on social work practice

5. A feminist perspective that acknowledges the oppression of women and the value of their unique point of view

6. A global perspective that acknowledges our interdependence and the existence of social and economic injustice worldwide

7. A critical perspective that allows for the examination of all forms of oppression and the development of strategies for change

The empowerment approach provides a framework with a value and knowledge base, practice principles and techniques within which a social worker can operate in a range of roles from direct service provider to broker/coordinator to system developer and advocate within all system levels.

From the personal dimension, an empowerment perspective directs the practitioner to work with clients in such a way as to develop their sense of mastery, competence and control, and to serve as a broker or facilitator of services and resources that are made available to clients. The social worker acknowledges the power differential in the client worker relationship and works to balance it by supporting the client's problem solving and coping capacities. The strengths perspective, discussed below, with its focus on client competence and client worker collaboration, supports and enhances feelings and self experience of agency and power. As discussed later in the chapter, an ego psychological approach can also help the social worker assess client strength and adaptation and shape interventions that are supportive of further growth and mastery. Thus, at the personal level, empowerment means "the development of a more positive and potent sense of self" (Lee, 2000a; p. 224) and can be a powerful tool for engaging with a client at the micro level of intervention.

Interpersonal empowerment refers to our ability to influence others. This ability is influenced by social power, which is derived from social status and from access to resources for personal development and for securing new positions (Miley et al., 2001). Social work mezzo level interventions from an empowerment perspective include raising consciousness regarding oppression, challenging and reshaping current societal ascriptions of power based on race, gender, and socioeconomic status, and providing clients with knowledge, skills and tools to grow and develop their capacities. At this level, empowerment translates into "the construction of knowledge and capacity for more critical comprehension of social and political realities of one's environment" (Lee, 2000a, p. 224).

The vulnerable, oppressed, and impoverished populations social workers serve often experience stark social and political realities and lack of access to resources. A key component of empowerment, and thus intervention from this perspective, also involves changing such unresponsive structures. This is the political dimension of empowerment. At this macro level, social workers can help clients examine their social and political realities, and advocate for and facilitate systemic changes. Political empowerment involves "the cultivation of resources and strategies, or more functional competence, for attainment of personal and collective social goals, or liberation" (Lee, 2000a, p. 224). Paradoxically, as Simon has stated (1990, p. 32):

> The one function that social workers...cannot perform for another person is that of empowerment. Empowerment is a reflexive activity, a process capable of being initiated and sustained only by the agent or subject who seeks power or self determination. Others can only aid and abet in this empowerment process. They do so by providing a climate, a relationship, resources, and procedural means through which people can enhance their own lives.

The Strengths Perspective

One way of abetting the empowerment process is through use of a strengths perspective. As its name suggests, and in keeping with the core social work values of fostering social justice and the dignity and worth of the person, the strengths perspective directs social workers to focus on the capacities and competencies of the client, rather than on the weaknesses, vulnerabilities and problems which sometimes are the object of professional assessment and intervention. According to Saleebey (1992), six principles are central to the strengths perspective, and guide the process of assessment and intervention from this stance:

1. Respect for Clients

The basic stance of the strengths perspective and, indeed, social work, is respect for the dignity and worth of the individual, and the provision of service with integrity and competence. Clients must be viewed and respected as having abilities, talents and desires that deserve to be recognized and allowed to unfold. This base of respect and recognition of worth is a powerful way to engage a client.

2. Clients Have Many Strengths

Clients possess a reservoir of potential and knowledge of their own experience, what they need, and what they want, which social workers must be skilled at eliciting and employing in their clients' service.

3. Client Motivation is Based on Developing Client Strengths

In the strengths perspective the emphasis is on the resilience and strength that clients have shown in surviving past painful experiences, and on harnessing their resourcefulness for further development. The strengths perspective focuses on fomenting hope and motivating clients to grow. Clients often have experienced a very different message, which is that nothing can change and that they are not capable of impacting their own lives.

4. The Social Worker is a Collaborator with the Client

The essence of the strengths perspective is viewing the client as most knowledgeable about his or her wants, needs and capacities. Thus, the social worker is a partner in the collaborative process of achieving client goals. There is a conscious effort to reduce the power differential between client and social worker by underscoring that the client, just like the social worker, has expertise in certain areas, namely his or her experience, and that the helping relationship is a collaborative and reciprocal partnership.

5. *Avoiding the Victim Mindset*

Unlike some models of professional assessment and intervention which emphasize the problem and do not take into account the role of the environment on the creation and perpetuation of the problem, the strengths perspective focuses on understanding how the environment causes problems, and also on how resources in the environment, coupled with client strengths, can be used to address it.

6. *Any Environment is Full of Resources*

All environments, even the harshest, have resources which are frequently unidentified and unexplored. Social workers must help their clients, whether an individual, family, group, organization or community, identify and access these existing, perhaps untapped resources, which can include knowledge, concrete services, time, and support. Social workers also have a professional responsibility to advocate for greater social justice, so that the range, availability, and quality of resources are continually expanded.

In summary, a strengths perspective views people as having significant, untapped reservoirs of mental, physical, emotional, social, and spiritual abilities and assumes a capacity for continued growth and development (Weick, Rapp, Sullivan, & Kisthardt, 1989). A strengths perspective moves the focus from problems to challenges, from pathology to strength, and from the past to the future (Miley et al., 2001). This framework aims to connect people to societal resources, and to increase the responsiveness of institutions to human needs. In these ways, the strengths perspective offers social workers an approach that operationalizes the core values of the social work profession.

Ego Psychology

Ego psychology is a theory of human functioning and behavior that provides a way of thinking about the mastery and adaptation of the individual to his or her environment. In this way, ego psychology interlocks with a systems approach and the strengths and empowerment perspectives previously discussed. The concept of the ego arose out of Freud's structural theory, in which he posited that there exist structures within the mind comprising the human psyche that are in conflict with each other. These structures include the id, the ego, and the superego (Freud, 1961).

According to Freud, the id is the source and repository of sexual and aggressive impulses or drives, is guided by the desire to experience pleasure, and thus is not directly influenced by morality, reality, logic or social convention. The superego comprises internalized moral beliefs and prohibitions. The ego mediates conflicts between the id, superego, and external society, and maintains psychological cohesion and stability.

Subsequent theorists such as Anna Freud (1936) and Heinz Hartmann (1939) greatly expanded the concept of the ego to address the central role it plays in organizing mental functions and in adapting to the external environment and the social and cultural context in which the individual develops and functions. Thus, ego psychology provides a theoretical framework for understanding human development, capacity, and adaptation, and for repairing the effects of compromised development through facilitation of a better fit between the individual and the external environment (Goldstein, 1995).

The following constitute the fundamental tenets of ego psychology, as summarized by Goldstein (1995):

1. People are born with the capacity to cope with and shape their environment to maximize adaptive functioning. These capacities for coping and adaptation are contained in the ego.

2. The ego can function autonomously, but it can be impacted by internal drives.

3. Ego functions are innate, and develop as a result of maturation and interaction between an individual's biopsychosocial makeup and the environment. Some of the ego functions include *reality testing*, the capacity for objective evaluation of the external world, as defined in particular sociocultural and historical context; *judgment*, the capacity to reach reasonable conclusions about what is appropriate behavior, and the consequences of actions; *regulation and control of drives, affects, and impulses*, which refers to the ability to modulate, delay, inhibit, or control the expression of impulses and affects in accord with reality and thus leads to adaptive functioning; and *thought processes*, the capacity to perceive and attend to stimuli, concentrate, anticipate, symbolize, remember, and reason.

4. Ego development occurs sequentially in the context of having basic needs met, identifying with others, learning, mastering developmental tasks, and coping with internal needs and external conditions and expectations.

5. The ego negotiates between internal needs and conflicts and the individual in his or her environment. It can use a variety of defenses, or mechanisms that protect an individual from anxiety by keeping intolerable or unacceptable impulses or threats from conscious awareness. Some examples of defenses include *denial*, in which the unconscious literally deletes from awareness an unpleasant or anxiety provoking reality; *repression*, in which the disturbing material is removed from consciousness or prevented from becoming conscious; and *intellectualization*, the avoidance of feeling by focusing on thinking. Some defenses are more adaptive than others.

6. Ego development occurs in the context of a social environment that may include conditions such as racism, poverty, or oppression that can impair adaptation and coping.

7. Problems in functioning and adaptation can be understood as possible deficits in the ego's capacity to cope, as deficits within the

environment and/or as a poor fit between the individual's needs and what the environment can offer.

Ego psychology provides a framework for assessing the level of functioning, coping, and mastery of an individual. It also views the fit between an individual and his or her environment as potentially fostering or impeding adaptive capacities. Finally, it provides a guide to intervention with both the individual and the environment that increases the individual's adaptation and sense of competence. This is done through ego supportive techniques, designed to restore, maintain, or strengthen adaptive functioning, ego modifying approaches, designed to alter basic personality patterns (Goldstein, 1995, 1996), or interventions within the environment to improve its fit with the individual's needs.

Summary

The systems, strengths, and empowerment perspectives and ego psychological theory discussed in this chapter each guide engagement, assessment, problem identification, and intervention planning, implementation, and evaluation in different ways, all congruent with a generalist approach to practice and the values of the social work profession. Chapter 4 describes a knowledge base specific to intervention in situations of crisis, disaster, and trauma.

Chapter 4

A Knowledge Base for Intervention in Crisis, Disaster, and Trauma

In order to apply the concepts and skills of generalist practice described in Chapters 2 and 3 to the events of September 11, it is necessary to have an understanding of the various ways in which crisis, disaster, and trauma affect individuals, families, groups, organizations, and communities. This chapter provides an introduction to, and an overview of, salient concepts relevant to theories of crisis, disaster, and trauma. In addition, it identifies and reviews common cognitive, emotional, and physical reactions to disaster and trauma as well as the signs and symptoms of Post Traumatic Stress Disorder (PTSD). This introduction and overview of key concepts regarding crisis, disaster, and trauma will provide a theoretical foundation in order to further understand the various practice examples that will be presented and discussed in Chapters 5 through 7.

Key Elements of Crisis Theory

Crisis is defined by Hoff (2001) as "an acute emotional upset arising from situational, developmental, or sociocultural sources and resulting in a temporary inability to cope by means of one's usual problem solving devices" (p. 4). Parad and Parad (1990) expand upon this definition by describing a crisis as "…an upset in a steady state, a turning point leading to better or worse, a disruption or breakdown in a person's or family's normal or usual pattern of functioning" (pp. 3 4).

Consistent with these definitions, Ell (1996) outlines the basic assumptions and tenets underlying crisis theory. According to Ell, these basic assumptions include the following:

- During crisis, individuals frequently experience a state of acute emotional disequilibrium, which is marked by physical symptoms, cognitive impairment, and social disorganization.

- The state of acute situational distress that accompanies a crisis upsets an individual's usual steady state. It is important to emphasize that this state of disequilibrium is not a pathological condition. Moreover, crises can happen to anyone at any time of life.

- During the state of disequilibrium that accompanies a crisis, individuals will naturally strive to return to a state of homeostasis or balance by mobilizing personal, familial, social, and environmental supports.

- While struggling to return to the previous state of homeostasis, individuals experience a time limited state of psychological, emotional, and, possibly, physical vulnerability that can be extremely difficult and distressing.

- During the heightened state of vulnerability that accompanies a crisis, individuals are often more receptive to and better able to utilize professional intervention.

- After the resolution of a crisis, individuals return to a state of functioning that may be either the same as, better, or worse than the original state of equilibrium prior to the crisis.

Two words that are commonly associated with crises are *danger* and *opportunity* (Hoff, 2001; Parad & Parad, 1990). The dangers that are associated with crises are clearly illustrated by states of disequilibrium, vulnerability, and extreme distress that frequently occur during these times. Although it may initially be difficult to identify opportunities that are inherent during crisis situations, individuals frequently discover previously unknown or underutilized strengths and resources within themselves or their support systems which result in unexpected opportunities for growth and development (Parad & Parad, 1990).

The Phases of a Crisis

Golan (1978) referred to the "crisis situation" (p. 7) as a predictable sequence of events that takes place in a crisis. This sequence of events includes a process in which one's state of equilibrium is thrown into a state of disequilibrium. With the successful resolution of the crisis, one returns to the original state of equilibrium. According to Golan, the five components of the *crisis situation* include the *hazardous event*, *vulnerable state*, *precipitating factor*, *state of active crisis*, and *reintegration* or *crisis resolution* (p.63 64). Golan described these five components in the following way:

The Hazardous Event

The hazardous event is a specific stressful event, which occurs to an individual who is in a state of relative stability. This event is a starting point, marking a change in the previous state of stability, which can also initiate a chain of events to further disrupt the equilibrium. Hazardous events can be anticipated and predictable, such as maturational events during developmental life stages (for example, adolescence or old age), or unanticipated and unexpected, including sudden death, loss of a job, or a disaster, like that of September 11.

The Vulnerable State

The vulnerable state is the idiosyncratic way in which individuals respond to the hazardous event both at the time it occurs as well as in the future. The vulnerable state can include a wide range of reactions, such as anxiety, depression, mourning, shame, guilt, anger, and cognitive or perceptual confusion, as well as feelings of hope, challenge, and excitement.

The Precipitating Factor

The precipitating factor is the "straw that breaks the camel's back" (Golan, p.66), or the factor in a chain of events that converts the vulnerable state into a state of disequilibrium. While in some cases the precipitating factor activates a previous vulnerable state caused by a prior hazardous event, in other cases, a precipitating factor will be the same as the hazardous event. For example, for some individuals, the September 11 disaster *activated* a vulnerable state created by a previous hazardous event, while for others, the September 11 disaster *was* the hazardous event. These differing experiences will be illustrated with case examples in Chapter 5.

The Active Crisis State

The state of active crisis describes the state of disequilibrium that occurs once the individual's previous homeostatic coping mechanisms have broken down. The state of active crisis is typically considered to be time limited, often described as four to six weeks, during which the individual experiences predictable responses including physical, emotional, and cognitive imbalance as well as preoccupation with the events which led to the crisis. During the state of active crisis, since the individual's previous defensive and coping mechanisms are ineffective, he or she is typically highly motivated to accept and utilize assistance. Thus, a minimal amount of focused assistance can be more useful during this time than more extensive efforts during times in which individuals are not as accessible to help.

Reintegration or Crisis Resolution

During the initial resolution of the active state of crisis, individuals struggle to master both a cognitive perception of what has occurred as well as both the release and acceptance of feelings related to the crisis. In the final stage of reintegration, the individual develops new patterns of coping, including improved access to and use of helping efforts, as well as identification and utilization of supports in the environment.

Disaster Theory

Golan applied her understanding of the phases of crisis situations in order to specify the events that take place in times of disaster. According to this theory, disaster is defined as "a collective stress situation in which many members of a social system fail to receive expected conditions of life, such as safety of the physical environment, protection from attack, provision of food, shelter, and income, and the guidance and information necessary to carry on normal activities" (Golan, 1978, p. 125).

Siporin (quoted in Golan, 1978) further elaborates upon Golan's definition of disaster by pointing out that a "disaster can engender severe crisis in that it threatens self images and identities, life goals and values, and the structure of social systems. It calls for greatly extended or restricted functioning for which customary coping patterns are, for the most part, inadequate. Both individuals and systems become disequilibrated and dysfunctional" (p.126).

Phases of Traumatic Stress Reactions in a Disaster

There are three predictable phases following a disaster—Impact, Recoil and Rescue, and Recovery phases (Hoff, 2001; Raphael, 2000). The following descriptions summarize these phases:

Impact Phase

During the impact phase, victims are experiencing the reality of the disaster and are concerned with the immediate present. Common reactions during the impact phase can range from remaining calm and organized to becoming shocked and confused, or becoming hysterical and paralyzed with fear (Hoff, 2001). In the aftermath of a disaster, victims are often surprised that they are able to function as well as they do during the impact phase.

Recoil and Rescue Phase

Rescue activities begin during the Recoil and Rescue phase. There are a wide range of physical and emotional reactions, including numbness; denial or shock; flashbacks and nightmares; grief reactions to loss; anger; despair; sadness; and hopelessness (Raphael, 2000). In addition, for those who have survived the disaster, there may be feelings of relief and elation, which may be difficult to accept in the context of the overall destruction and devastation that has occurred, engendering survival guilt (Lifton, 1982).

Recovery Phase

The recovery phase begins in the weeks after the impact phase and continues through the prolonged period in which individuals and the community face the complex task of returning to a new state of "normal" and attempt to regain a pre crisis state of equilibrium. The initial stage of the recovery phase is often referred to as a honeymoon period in which there is an outpouring of altruism and interpersonal connectedness in response to the disaster. Following this initial stage, a period of disillusionment frequently occurs in which realities of the devastation and loss brought about by the disaster must be faced and resolved (Raphael, 2000).

Common and Normative Responses to Trauma

Emotional, Cognitive, Physical, and Interpersonal Responses

Before describing disorders that can occur as a result of trauma, it is important to be familiar with the range of common and normative emotional, cognitive, physical and interpersonal responses to extreme trauma. Many people responded to the September 11 disaster with a variety of the following behaviors and reactions:

Emotional Effects	
▪ Shock	▪ Emotional numbing
▪ Terror	▪ Helplessness
▪ Irritability	▪ Loss of pleasure derived from familiar activities
▪ Blame	
	▪ Difficulty feeling happy
▪ Anger	
	▪ Difficulty experiencing loving feelings
▪ Guilt	
▪ Grief or sadness	

Physical Effects	
▪ Fatigue, exhaustion	▪ Reduced immune response
▪ Insomnia	▪ Headaches
▪ Cardiovascular strain	▪ Gastrointestinal upset
▪ Startle response	▪ Increased or decreased appetite
▪ Hyperarousal	▪ Decreased libido
▪ Increased physical pain	▪ Vulnerability to illness

Cognitive Effects	
▪ Impaired concentration	▪ Decreased self esteem
▪ Impaired decision making ability	▪ Decreased self efficacy
▪ Memory impairment	▪ Self blame
▪ Disbelief	▪ Intrusive thoughts/memories
▪ Confusion	▪ Worry
▪ Nightmares	▪ Dissociation (e.g., tunnel vision, dreamlike or "spacey" feeling)

Interpersonal Effects	
▪ Increased relational conflict	▪ Decreased satisfaction
▪ Social withdrawal	▪ Distrust
▪ Reduced relational intimacy	▪ Externalization of blame
▪ Alienation	▪ Externalization of vulnerability
▪ Impaired work performance	▪ Feeling abandoned/rejected
▪ Impaired school performance	▪ Overprotectiveness

(http://www.ncptsd.org/facts/disasters/fs_effects_disaster.html, 12/27/01)

Post Traumatic Stress Disorder

While the behaviors and responses described above are normative and expectable reactions to a disaster situation such as that of September 11, if they do not diminish, or if they interfere with functioning, Post Traumatic Stress Disorder (PTSD) may be diagnosed. Post Traumatic Stress Disorder is a syndrome that can occur when one is exposed to extreme traumatic stress. According to the Diagnostic and Statistical Manual of Mental Disorders (DSM IV TR, 2000), a diagnosis of Post Traumatic Stress Disorder can be given when the following criteria are met:

- There has been exposure to a traumatic stressor or event
- Re experiencing symptoms are present
- Avoidance and numbing symptoms are present
- Symptoms of increased arousal are present

- The above symptoms have been present for a duration of at least one month

- The above symptoms cause significant distress or impairment in functioning

Exposure to a traumatic stressor

In order to be diagnosed with PTSD, an individual must have been exposed to a traumatic event in which both of the following were present:

(1)   The individual experienced, witnessed, or learned about an event that involved actual or threatened death or serious injury, or a threat to the physical integrity of one's self or others.

(2)   The individual's response to the traumatic event involved intense fear, helplessness, or horror.

Some severely traumatized individuals may dissociate during exposure to a traumatic stressor or have a blunted response as a result of avoidance and numbing. In some cases, the intense emotional response to the traumatic stressor may not occur until considerable time has elapsed after the traumatic event.

Presence of re experiencing symptoms

One set of PTSD symptoms includes persistent and distressing re experiencing of the traumatic event in one or more ways. These re experienced memories of the trauma are unwanted, occur involuntarily, elicit distressing emotions, and disrupt the individual's functioning. One or more of the following re experiencing symptoms must be present in order for the diagnosis of Post Traumatic Stress Disorder to be made:

- Recurrent and intrusive images, thoughts, or perceptions of the event

- Recurrent distressing dreams of the traumatic event

- Acting or feeling as though the traumatic event were recurring (reliving the experience through illusions, hallucinations, dissociative flashbacks)

- Intense psychological distress to internal or external cues that symbolize or resemble an aspect of the traumatic event

- Physiological reactivity to external or internal cues that symbolize or resemble an aspect of the traumatic event

Presence of avoidance and numbing symptoms

A second set of PTSD symptoms include persistent avoidance of stimuli which are reminders associated with the trauma as well as general numbing of one's responses. Three or more of the following avoidance and numbing symptoms must be present in order to make a diagnosis of Post Traumatic Stress Disorder:

- Avoidance of thoughts, feelings, or conversations associated with the trauma

- Avoidance of activities, places, or people that arouse recollections of the trauma

- Inability to recall an important aspect of the trauma

- Markedly diminished interest or participation in previously enjoyed or significant activities

- Feelings of detachment or estrangement from others or restricted range of affect

- Sense of foreshortened future (e.g. the individual does not expect to have a career, marriage, children, or a normal life)

Presence of symptoms of increased arousal

A third set of PTSD symptoms includes persistent symptoms of increased arousal that were not present before exposure to the traumatic event. Two or more of the following symptoms of increased arousal must be present in order to make a diagnosis of Post Traumatic Stress Disorder:

- Difficulty falling or staying asleep (including the presence of nightmares)

- Irritability or outbursts of anger

- Difficulty with concentration or completing tasks (due to intrusive thoughts about the traumatic event)

- Hypervigilance (in an effort to prevent recurrence of the traumatic event)

- Exaggerated startle response

The presence of symptoms for duration of more than one month

The symptoms of re experiencing the event, avoidance and numbing, and increased arousal must be present for more than one month. It should be noted that a diagnosis of *Acute Post Traumatic Stress Disorder* is given if the duration of symptoms is less than three months. A diagnosis of *Chronic Post Traumatic Stress Disorder* is given if the duration of the symptoms is three months or more. A diagnosis of *Post Traumatic Stress Disorder with Delayed Onset* is given if the onset of symptoms is at least 6 months after the stressor (DSMIV TR, 2000).

The symptoms must cause significant distress or impairment of functioning

The symptoms described above must cause clinically significant distress or impairment in social, occupational, or other important areas of functioning, such as the ability to engage in and enjoy recreational and/or leisure activities.

The Professional's Role in Disaster Work: Crisis Intervention

Many of the professionals who volunteered to assist in the aftermath of September 11 did so in the dual capacity of professional helpers and individuals who were themselves affected in many different ways. Struck with their own grief, mourning, and shock, they struggled to make sense out of the extremely disturbing events. Moreover, they attempted to recover from the effects of the disaster as quickly as possible in order to begin to help others.

Crisis intervention is defined by Parad and Parad (1990) as "a process for actively influencing psychosocial functioning during a period of disequilibrium in order to alleviate the immediate impact of disruptive stressful events and to help mobilize the capabilities and resources of the persons affected by the crisis" (p. 4). Accordingly, the goals of crisis intervention are to deal with the immediate crisis and strengthen the individual's coping capabilities for the future.

As indicated by this definition, crisis intervention is consistent with principles of the strengths perspective discussed in Chapter 3. Specifically, there is an emphasis on mobilizing strengths and capacities in order to help the client system, that is, the individual, family, group, organization or community, return to the pre crisis level of functioning. Ego psychological techniques can also be useful in crisis intervention to assess the individual's level of functioning, coping, and adaptation. An empowerment perspective is also helpful in utilizing the client's inner and environmental resources.

Generalist practitioners are guided by several important practice principles that are consistent with strengths and empowerment approaches and ego psychological theory, when intervening in situations of crisis and disaster. As described by Ell (1996), these practice principles include:

- In the aftermath of a disaster, help is provided immediately, including outreach to populations who may not otherwise seek assistance.

- Interventions at the time of the disaster are time limited and brief.

- The practitioner takes an active, often directive, stance in helping efforts. It is often necessary for the practitioner to engage quickly and explore sensitive and potentially difficult areas such as suicidality and issues related to death and dying.

- The primary goal of intervention is the reduction of symptoms and a return to the earlier state of equilibrium.

- Interventions often include a combination of counseling to handle emotional concerns, provision of practical information and tangible support, and the mobilization of social and environmental support systems.

- The expression of feelings, symptoms, and worries is encouraged.

- Strategies for problem solving and effective coping are encouraged and supported to help the individual return to a state of equilibrium.

- Use of strengths, capacities, and resources within the individual and the environment are a central focus of interventions.

Assessment

A key aspect of generalist intervention in the context of disaster is the implementation of a prompt and thorough assessment. Cohen (1990, p. 283) provides a useful framework for the biopsychosocial and cultural assessment of each individual's reaction to the sudden and intense impact of a disaster that includes the following dimensions:

1. The individual's personality structure

2. The individual's age, gender, ethnicity, and economic status

3. The individual's usual coping style (including adaptive and nonadaptive defenses)

4. The intensity of the stressors caused by the disaster

5. The available and appropriate "fit" between the individual's needs and availability of support systems

6. The extent of personal loss suffered

7. The availability of relief emergency resources

Distinctions Between Crisis Intervention and Psychotherapy

Parad and Parad (1990) point out that crisis intervention is not synonymous with psychotherapy. Many experienced clinicians and psychotherapists who participated in the massive volunteer response to the events of September 11 learned that the services required in this disaster were quite different from traditional counseling services. The mental health volunteers needed to learn about new ways to deliver crisis intervention and disaster mental health services. As Taffel (2001, p. 24) described it:

> Everyone would be required to set aside familiar ways of doing therapy— psychodynamic, self psychology, strategic or family systems work. They would be providing short term disaster counseling to victims in the initial stage of shock, disorientation and biological deregulation that follows devastating collective trauma.

The following descriptions by Taffel (2001), of mental health volunteer work following September 11, convey principles of client centered generalist practice and crisis intervention:

> Absolutely key to this whole effort was the willingness of clinicians to set aside their familiar and comfortable ways of working—temporarily relinquish their own clinical paradigms, theories, modalities and techniques—and truly give clients what they wanted and asked for in the moment, when they asked for it. (p. 39)

> Volunteers would need to follow the client's lead. That might mean replaying what happened or helping someone make a decision about where to stay that night. The work would require careful pacing. A defended, guarded person processing the trauma, for instance, could not be pushed and probably could not stand too much sympathy. We had to say it in 10 different ways: we would not promote insight, catharsis or uncovering. We were only there to help people regain some mastery over eating and sleeping and basic self regulation. (p. 24)

Summary

In the aftermath of September 11, consistent with principles of crisis theory, interventions focused on reducing symptoms related to the trauma and providing support. Specific intervention strategies included education, clarification, and reassurance about normative, expectable reactions to this trauma in order to reduce intense anxiety and fear and to encourage the expression of feelings and worries. Interventions also focused on providing practical information, tangible support, and assistance to help people mobilize and further develop support systems. In addition to these interventions, rapid but thorough assessments of pre and post disaster functioning were necessary, in all cases, to identify individuals who might need further professional assistance.

Chapters 5, 6, and 7 provide detailed examples of interventions with individuals, families, groups, organizations, and the larger New York City community undertaken in the wake of September 11. These examples further illustrate the crisis intervention practice principles and roles assumed by generalist social work practitioners discussed in this chapter.

PART III

OPERATIONALIZING GENERALIST
SOCIAL WORK PRACTICE
IN THE WAKE OF DISASTER:
CASE STUDIES

Chapter 5

Micro Level Generalist Practice:
Interventions with
Individuals, Families, and Groups

As discussed, a distinguishing characteristic of generalist practice is the differential application of a wide repertoire of skills at varying system levels depending on context, setting, and need, all of which are ascertained through a comprehensive assessment. This chapter presents social work practice vignettes with individuals, families, and groups in the aftermath of September 11. The vignettes, drawn from a variety of settings, highlight the multiple roles social workers assume and the varying levels at which practice is directed.

Direct Practice with Individuals

University Gymnasium: Outreach Services

The setting for the first practice vignette is an urban university gymnasium where outreach services were provided to students, on a drop in basis, immediately following the disaster. Outreach services included recreational and social opportunities, food, free telephones, and informal counseling services provided by volunteer mental health staff. In addition to these services, many students who were displaced from dormitories close to the World Trade Center were provided with cots set up in the gymnasium. Outreach services that are immediately and universally accessible and provided in an informal and natural setting are an essential early intervention following a disaster (Golan, 1978; Parad & Parad, 1990).

Andrea

Two days after the disaster, Andrea, an 18 year old, Irish American college freshman who had arrived in New York City a week earlier from Atlanta, came to the gymnasium from her dormitory ten blocks away to speak with a counselor. While she stated she was "still in shock and afraid," Andrea was able to calmly discuss the events since the attacks.

Andrea's primary concern was an argument she just had by telephone with her mother who called from Atlanta. Extremely concerned about Andrea's safety in New York City, Andrea's mother wanted her to visit distant relatives in a suburban area for the weekend so that she could get out of the city. Andrea did not want to leave the city, instead she wanted to stay in the dormitory with her roommate and friends, with whom she had developed a strong and supportive bond in the past two days through their common experience of the disaster.

Following the model of crisis assessment described in Chapter 4, the social worker first explored Andrea's response to the hazardous event, in this case, the terrorist attacks. Andrea displayed strengths in coping with the disaster, including spending time with newfound friends, seeking out adults in the dormitory, and attempting to do schoolwork, despite difficulties concentrating.

Next, the social worker assessed Andrea's baseline functioning before the disaster by exploring her recent past. Andrea revealed that in her last year of high school she had experienced a period of depression marked by isolation from friends and a loss of interest in activities, such as competitive swimming. When the depression worsened, Andrea confided in her mother, who helped her obtain counseling and medication. As a result of this past experience, Andrea's parents initially did not want her to move to New York City and now were fearful that she would return to this earlier state of depression.

In her assessment of Andrea's current functioning, the social worker learned that as a result of her past counseling, Andrea was able to cope with her feelings effectively and utilize existing support systems. She further assessed that as an adolescent recently away from home,

Andrea was actively mastering normative developmental tasks of autonomy and separation. Moreover, while Andrea respected her mother's desire to protect her and wished to comply with her mother's request, at the same time she wanted to exercise her developing sense of competence and independence by remaining with her new friends. For Andrea, it was more stressful to leave the city for an unknown location to be with relatives she did not know, than to stay in the city with a group of peers with whom she had bonded and felt comfortable.

The social worker assessed that Andrea was coping well with the stresses of the disaster. Since the problematic situation appeared to exist between Andrea and her mother, the social worker considered the importance of intervening directly with Andrea's mother. The social worker suggested that together they call Andrea's mother in order to further assess her mother's concerns and help her understand the circumstances in New York City following the disaster. Thus, the intervention involved the family system as well as the individual.

In speaking with Andrea's mother by telephone, the social worker more fully understood her concerns. Moreover, she was able to help Andrea's mother appreciate the fact that despite her prior difficulties, Andrea had used good judgment in seeking help and was utilizing existing support services within the dormitory. In addition, she was able to help Andrea's mother put her concerns into perspective by pointing out that many students wished to stay in the city where they felt that people understood, while those who had not experienced the disaster as directly might not. The social worker further conveyed to Andrea's mother that her daughter would feel safer remaining in the city as she felt more threatened with the idea of finding her way to an unknown location and being with people she did not know well.

Andrea's mother expressed gratitude for the opportunity to speak with another adult who could help her understand what her daughter was experiencing. In addition, she was relieved to know that support services were available to Andrea at all times. Andrea, her mother, and the worker collaboratively developed a plan to evaluate how Andrea felt the next day to determine if she might go for a day trip to her relatives rather than spend the entire weekend. Andrea called the social worker the next day, reported that she was feeling better, and that she had decided to visit her relatives for the day. Andrea was also interested in joining a peer support group that was established in her dormitory and agreed to contact the counseling center if she felt she needed any further assistance.

Discussion

In this case, guided by the theories and techniques of crisis intervention, the social worker made a clinical assessment in order to determine Andrea's ability to cope with the disaster. Moreover, by utilizing a systems perspective, the social worker was able to identify where in the system intervention was needed. In keeping with a crisis model, interventions were active, directive, and concrete. While the focus was on the current crisis, a thorough assessment was made of both present and past functioning and coping capacities.

The social worker assumed multiple roles, including *crisis counselor* for both Andrea and her mother, *advocate* and *mediator* by facilitating communication between Andrea and her mother, *educator* to both Andrea and her mother regarding the expectable reactions in response to the disaster, and *broker* of services, by linking Andrea to the ongoing support groups that were being provided in her dormitory.

University Counseling Center

In the week following the disaster, counseling and support services were relocated from the gymnasium to the university's Counseling Center in order to provide privacy, continuity, and structure that was not possible in the gymnasium. As in the gymnasium, outreach services at the counseling center were made easily and universally accessible to all students through walk in intake appointments. The following three vignettes, drawn from social work practice in this setting, illustrate a range of post disaster reactions and needs, including the physical manifestation of symptoms, the difficulty the disaster posed even for students with no previous history of trauma, and the ways that significant prior trauma impacts an individual's capacity to cope with a new stressor. In each situation, the generalist practitioner needed well developed assessment and diagnostic skills, the capacity to choose appropriate interventions, and the ability to implement these interventions promptly.

Don

Don is a 24 year old, Italian American man from Providence, Rhode Island. He is the eldest of three children, with a 19 year old sister who is a college sophomore and a 17 year old brother who is a high school student. Don's mother is an interior designer and his father is an accountant.

Don excelled in college both academically and socially. During his senior year he was diagnosed with irritable bowel syndrome for which he takes medication and follows a special diet. Don moved to New York City and worked for one year as a teacher's aide before beginning a graduate program in Anthropology in September, 2001.

Don came to the Counseling Center complaining of a flare up of his irritable bowel symptoms, as well as anxiety and depression, which he attributed to September 11. In the first session, two weeks after the disaster, Don reported that he experienced insomnia and nightmares, especially a recurring one in which an airplane flew through his abdomen.

In conducting a biopsychosocial assessment, the social worker gathered information about Don's current and past functioning, including the quality of familial and social relationships. Through this exploration, the worker learned that last February Don had met Karen, his current girlfriend. Karen is Jewish, and Don's Catholic family does not approve of the relationship. Don was angry at his parents and troubled by their intolerance. As a result, there had been tension between Don and his parents and he had been reluctant to reach out to them for support in the aftermath of the disaster. In addition, while Don excelled academically as an undergraduate, he was feeling overwhelmed by the responsibility and challenge of graduate coursework and was worried that he would not do well.

The social worker provided comprehensive interventions that addressed Don's medical, educational, familial, and social needs. Don had not sought medical care since his arrival in New York, relying instead on a renewable prescription from his previous doctor. The social worker referred Don to a gastroenterologist for further assessment of his medical needs and emphasized the importance of maintaining this linkage with ongoing medical care. In addition, she provided psychoeducation regarding expectable responses to disaster, including the ways in which physical symptoms can manifest, and normalized his experience. The social worker also helped Don understand how chronic stress related to his medical condition made him particularly vulnerable to additional stressors, such as the effects of the disaster and familial tensions. Together they discussed adaptive ways of coping with his stress, such as obtaining individual counseling, joining a support group in his dorm, and resuming his exercise and eating regimen.

The social worker provided Don with information about a range of available academic supports. During the course of individual counseling, Don also had the opportunity to discuss his strong feelings for Karen as well as anger and disappointment at his parents' lack of support of this relationship. Don discussed and role played with the social worker the issues that he wanted to raise with his parents. He then made plans to visit them over the Thanksgiving holiday to speak with them directly. Don reported that his nightmares disappeared several days after the second session and his physical symptoms lessened over the next few sessions. After four sessions Don terminated counseling, stating that he was feeling much better.

Discussion

While the disaster was the precipitating factor that led Don to access counseling services, by conducting a thorough assessment the social worker uncovered a previous vulnerable state which resulted from his chronic medical condition and the more recent disruption in his relationship with his parents. The social worker assumed a variety of roles in helping Don. Specifically, the practitioner *educated* Don regarding expectable reactions to stress, especially given his medical condition, provided *linkage* to a variety of services, including a medical doctor, academic support, and a peer support group, and *collaborated* with the doctor to convey her understanding of the ways in which Don's physical symptoms were manifestations of his emotional stress. The social worker was knowledgeable about the availability of ongoing support groups because, as a senior clinician, she was providing *training* and *consultation* to the group facilitators. Finally, the practitioner employed strengths and empowerment perspectives to support Don in exploring both his fears of graduate school and the strained relationship with his parents.

Maria

Maria is a 26 year old woman who moved to New York City from Argentina to attend a Masters program at a large urban university two weeks before the disaster. Maria came to the university's Counseling Center five weeks after the attacks complaining of acute and persistent anxiety related to September 11 that had increased as a result of repeated anthrax threats. Since the disaster, Maria had been receiving daily telephone calls from her parents in Argentina, requesting that she return home.

In conducting an assessment, the social worker learned that Maria had functioned well prior to the attacks and was making a good adjustment to her move to New York City. Maria had a stable background and family life without any history of trauma or problems, but her current support system in New York was limited to her two roommates and a cousin. As a result of her prior high functioning, as well as what she described as cultural prohibitions regarding mental health treatment, Maria was initially quite reluctant to seek help.

Since Maria was preoccupied with her safety, she was not able to concentrate on her schoolwork, her sleep was disturbed, and her appetite had decreased markedly. While she considered going away to stay with relatives for the weekend in Boston, she wondered whether she would be safe traveling by train. Her overarching concern was whether or not she should remain enrolled in a one year Masters program, as she worried that, given her distress resulting from the disaster, she would not be able to focus on her studies and maximize her learning.

Interventions in the intake session focused on an assessment of Maria's current and past functioning as well as on concrete problem solving and decision making regarding Maria's immediate concerns. After conducting a thorough and focused assessment of current and past functioning, strengths, and coping mechanisms, the social worker was able to help Maria manage her anxiety for the upcoming weekend. She did this by helping Maria consider the pros and cons of going away for the weekend. By the end of the session, Maria had decided that it would be helpful for her to go away for a few days in order to be in a supportive environment with relatives outside of New York City.

In addition, the social worker was able to help Maria consider and develop ways to structure and manage her schoolwork. Through a discussion about her current assignments and upcoming deadlines for these, Maria was able to develop a manageable plan for completion of her work which included speaking with her professors to obtain extensions, as needed. The social worker also helped Maria arrange a meeting with the director of her Masters program in order to obtain further information about her options for leaving the program and resuming it the next year.

Finally, the social worker helped Maria develop a plan to attend short term crisis counseling which could help her decide whether or not she would remain in New York to complete the Masters program. She pointed out that if Maria decided to stay in the program, the short term counseling could help her develop strategies to manage her anxiety and build a support system in the city. Maria left the intake session with an appointment to meet with a staff social worker three days later who would be able to help her continue problem solving around all of the issues she raised in this initial session and make long range plans regarding her participation in the Masters program.

Discussion

This is an illustration of intervention with a person experiencing the hazardous event, but with no preexisting vulnerable state. The social worker was able to readily mobilize Maria's strengths and resources in order to help her return to her previous high level of functioning. The social worker did this in her role as a *counselor*, helping Maria to discuss her concerns, an *educator*, by normalizing her reactions, and a *broker* of services by referring her to short term counseling.

Ursula

Ursula, a 28 year old Croatian full time graduate student nearing completion of her dissertation, was referred to the counseling center nine days after the disaster by her professor, who accompanied her to the intake appointment. Ursula presented in a state of acute anxiety and depression, stating that she had come to the appointment because she was concerned that she might hurt herself. Given the seriousness of the presenting problem, the social worker focused on engaging Ursula and began to conduct a thorough biopsychosocial assessment of her present and past functioning, with particular attention to current and past states of depression and suicidality.

The social worker began by exploring the precipitating events that led Ursula to this state of depression and suicidality. Ursula reported that she had been hospitalized three days before September 11 due to a spontaneous abortion. During her hospitalization, she had experienced unexpected medical complications which led to cardiac problems for which she was subsequently treated. Upon discharge, two days after the attacks, Ursula began to feel increasingly depressed, had recurrent thoughts about hurting herself, and had nightmares about the attacks on the World Trade Center.

Concerned about the level of depression that Ursula was reporting, the social worker wanted to specifically assess not only the immediate crisis of her suicidality, but also the history and course of her depression

71

and any other trauma she had experienced in the past. Through this focused assessment, the social worker learned that Ursula had moved to New York City five years earlier from the former Yugoslavia, where she had experienced the effects of war for many years. In addition to recounting her memories of living in a war torn country, Ursula reported that her father physically abused her on a daily basis between the ages of thirteen and eighteen. During the time of the abuse, Ursula became increasingly depressed and made two suicide gestures, including ingestion of pills and an attempt to cut her wrists with a razor. As a result of these gestures, Ursula was taken to an emergency room, but she did not receive any treatment for depression. The social worker became further concerned when Ursula reported hearing voices that told her to hurt herself.

Based on this assessment, the social worker's first priority was to develop a safety plan with Ursula that included an immediate referral for further psychiatric evaluation and ongoing mental health services. The social worker emphasized to Ursula that she was concerned about her safety and well being. In addition, she conveyed to Ursula understanding and empathy regarding the hardship and distress she had experienced in the past, both in her country of origin and within her family.

The social worker obtained a verbal contract from Ursula that she would not harm herself. She also discussed with Ursula her plan to consult with the center's psychiatrist about her depressive and suicidal symptoms so that she could help Ursula develop a follow up plan. Having secured Ursula's agreement, the social worker consulted with the psychiatrist, who agreed to provide a full psychiatric evaluation the following day, provided that a clear and firm safety plan was put in place for that evening.

Ursula agreed to involve her boyfriend in the plan to ensure her safety. The social worker called the boyfriend and requested that he come to the counseling center to review the plan and to pick Ursula up. In a joint session with Ursula and her boyfriend, the social worker and Ursula reviewed the safety plan that they had jointly developed, as well as the follow up plan. The safety plan specified the actions that Ursula would take if she again felt that she might hurt herself. These included speaking with her boyfriend about these feelings and, if they persisted, having the boyfriend bring Ursula directly to the hospital emergency room. Ursula and her boyfriend both agreed to this plan and Ursula was given appointments for the next day with a social worker for a complete intake assessment and with the staff psychiatrist for a full psychiatric evaluation. Finally, with Ursula's agreement, her professor, who was concerned about her safety and well being, was apprised of this plan. Ursula was responsive to the social worker's active, directive, and focused interventions and appeared relieved to have been able to express her fears and obtain help.

Discussion

In this complex case, the social worker utilized *direct practice skills* to conduct an in depth assessment of Ursula's depression, suicidality, history of abuse and neglect, and mental status. Based on this assessment, she developed a clear and firm plan to ensure the client's safety. The social worker further utilized skills in *interdisciplinary collaboration* by consulting with the psychiatrist regarding the client's medical and psychiatric needs. Through this consultation, she assessed the need for further psychiatric evaluation and follow up and provided the necessary *linkages* with ongoing psychiatric and mental health services. Finally, the social worker *collaborated* actively to *mobilize* the client's support system, her boyfriend and her professor, to help them understand the need for continued monitoring and treatment of her acute condition and to help ensure her participation in ongoing services.

Family Service Agency

Mrs. Kelvin

The following case example, which took place at a family service agency, illustrates the strong impact September 11 had even on people who were far from the disaster site and did not know anyone who perished or was injured. Alice Kelvin is an African American woman who is married and the mother of two grown children, one of whom recently had a baby. Mrs. Kelvin was able to seek services from a family service agency in a small rural New Jersey town because the agency was supported by a United Way fund to offer free counseling to any residents in the county affected by the September 11 disaster. This funding decision is an example of a macro level intervention resulting in the provision of micro level services.

When Mrs. Kelvin first met with the social worker she reported that she was "grief stricken." She had difficulty controlling her tears, and was physically shaking as a result of the anxiety engendered by the disaster, even three weeks after the event. She wasn't sleeping well and had lost ten pounds. She was particularly concerned about her strong reaction because she did not know anyone who was killed or injured. However, she had watched television coverage almost non stop. Mrs. Kelvin's husband is a truck driver who is often on the road, and because Mrs. Kelvin does not work, she had been alone most of the time. In her anxious state, Mrs. Kelvin stated that she was "starting to believe that he [her husband] prefers to be away from me, especially now that I am so over emotional and maybe having a nervous breakdown." Her son lives in Philadelphia and although her daughter lives within an hour's drive, "she is busy with her baby and I don't want to trouble her."

The social worker assessed that Mrs. Kelvin's current symptoms were significant and impairing her daily functioning. Of great concern was her isolation and lack of a support system. The treatment plan, arrived at collaboratively, included goals of reducing Mrs. Kelvin's anxiety, helping her develop adaptive coping mechanisms, and increasing her social support network.

After several sessions Mrs. Kelvin began to discuss her relationship with her husband and explore the reasons that she felt so unsupported by him. Employing a systems approach, the social worker raised the possibility of Mrs. Kelvin inviting her husband to a session in order to further explore these issues together. Mrs. Kelvin agreed to this suggestion and indicated that she would talk with her husband about this idea.

Discussion

As a *direct service provider,* the social worker offered a safe, consistent place for Mrs. Kelvin to talk about her fears and loneliness. In addition, she helped Mrs. Kelvin establish some adaptive coping responses, such as reaching out to friends, listening to music, and exercising. In her role as *broker* of services, the social worker referred Mrs. Kelvin to a psychiatrist for a medication evaluation because of the severity of her depressive symptoms. As a *psychoeducator*, the social worker provided information about expectable reactions to the attacks and more extreme responses, such as those Mrs. Kelvin was experiencing, which required professional attention. Using a systems approach, the social worker started where Mrs. Kelvin was, attending to her immediate concerns and needs, and then explored and intervened in other parts of the system, such as her relationship with her husband, which they both agreed needed attention.

Direct Practice with Families

School based Services

The Bell Family

Emily, a nine year old girl in the fifth grade, was the only child in her elementary school to lose a parent in the World Trade Center attacks. Her father worked as an accountant in one of the financial companies. Emily has two younger brothers, Daniel, aged 6, and Alex, aged 4. Emily had been absent from school for one week following the attacks on the World Trade Center, and upon returning to her classroom, she was aggressive and oppositional, fighting with her classmates and refusing to follow her teacher's directions. Emily's teacher had become increasingly impatient with her disruptive and attention seeking behavior and, by November, requested that Emily be removed from her class and placed elsewhere.

When Emily's aggressive outbursts continued in a new classroom, the principal asked a school based social worker to see her. The social worker contacted Emily's mother, Mrs. Bell, to request permission to see Emily and also to assess how the family was coping with Mr. Bell's death. Mrs. Bell reported that despite support from her extended family, synagogue and neighbors, she and the children were profoundly saddened and distressed by the devastating loss of Mr. Bell. In addition, she was concerned about financial matters, as the family had been dependent on her husband's income and she had little knowledge of or understanding about their financial status since her husband had taken care of all the family's financial needs.

Mrs. Bell was surprised that Emily was presenting behavior problems in school because at home she was sad and tearful while Alex was the child exhibiting the aggression. Moreover, her six year old son Daniel was expressing intense fears following September 11. Daniel had a history of anxiety, manifested in difficulty falling asleep and clinging behavior with his mother. Even before the disaster and the sudden loss of his father, he had been afraid of the dark, of elevators, of sleeping alone, of being separated from his mother, and of going anywhere by himself, including the bathroom. He always took his younger brother with him. Mrs. Bell felt that his fears stemmed from an incident when Daniel was three, in which he had choked on his food and nearly died. Despite Daniel's anxious behavior, the Bells had not sought professional help for him. However, just three days before, Daniel had told her, "It's not fair that I'm never going to grow up to be a dad, and that everyone else will be big, but I am going to die." This statement had frightened her. She had been thinking of calling someone for help as she was confused about the children's very different reactions and was feeling quite overwhelmed. Consequently, the social worker's phone call had come at a propitious time.

After listening to Mrs. Bell, the social worker suggested that she meet with her and the children. A series of sessions were set up at the school for the family to discuss their feelings around their loss. Mrs. Bell expressed appreciation that she could come there and not a mental health clinic, because she "didn't want to feel like she was crazy for having these feelings." The social worker normalized the range of responses the Bell family was experiencing as a result of this extremely traumatic event.

After a thorough assessment, the social worker recommended continued family counseling as well as further evaluations for Daniel and Emily, and referred Mrs. Bell to a nearby community mental health center for these services. The social worker also referred Mrs. Bell to the Family Assistance Center, described in Chapter 7, so that she could receive help dealing with her family's finances, insurance benefits, and other important legal and monetary matters. In addition, she contracted with Mrs. Bell to meet with the family to provide ongoing case management of these services.

The social worker assessed that the teachers and staff at the school were in need of psychoeducation regarding children's expectable reactions to trauma. She felt that if Emily's teacher had this information, she would have been better prepared to understand and deal with Emily's behavior, and perhaps Emily would not have sustained the further stress of being transferred from her classroom.

Based on her assessment of staff educational needs, the social worker collaborated with the principal and school psychologist to develop a two hour training session on children's responses to trauma that she conducted in the school auditorium for all school staff. Through this training, staff members were given an opportunity to discuss their own feelings about what had happened, and the reactions they observed in their students. Many of the staff were surprised that both themselves and their students were experiencing significant reactions to the disaster even though they had not been affected in the immediate way that Emily had been. In addition, the social worker provided specific strategies for school staff to help themselves and their students cope with the traumatic events.

Discussion

The social worker's handling of Emily's situation illustrates several key elements of a generalist practice approach. First, there were interventions with various systems and at several levels. The individual and family work with the Bells are examples of micro level interventions. The training held for school staff is an example of a mezzo level intervention. The Family Assistance Center, to which Mrs. Bell was referred, is an example of macro level service planning and delivery. Secondly, the social worker employed her skills in *engagement*, *assessment*, and *intervention* in working with each system at the varying levels. Third, the social worker assumed a variety of roles as *direct service provider* of individual and family services, *broker* in referring Mrs. Bell to various services, and *organizational consultant/developer* and *trainer* to school personnel.

Finally, the interventions were tailored to meet client needs based on setting and context. While initially the social worker began her interventions with Emily, it became apparent that the entire family required assistance. A systems approach allowed the social worker to identify the need for intervention in the wider school system as well, so that Emily's teacher would be more sensitive to her, and all school staff could respond to their colleagues and the students more effectively.

Direct Practice with Groups

Community based Organization

Grupo de Apoyo Esperanza: The Women's Support Group

Members of a long running support group for HIV positive women held at a grass roots community based organization serving the Latino community in a borough of New York City had increasingly been complaining of fear, anxiety, sleep disruption and physical aches following September 11. The paraprofessional facilitator of the group, Ms. Ponce, uncertain about how to proceed, sought consultation from a social worker. The social worker met with Ms. Ponce to discuss the situation and decide on a course of action. In order to obtain a more thorough understanding of the group's needs, the social worker decided to lead a psychoeducational session. This two hour session took place at the community center nearly three months after the attacks and was held in Spanish. There were nine women present, ranging in age from 28 to 56.

Translated materials developed by the Red Cross on common responses to trauma in adults and children (see Chapter 4) and coping techniques were distributed and reviewed. The group also discussed the special vulnerability of people already dealing with a serious psychosocial stressor such as HIV positive status. This informational format allowed the women to gradually discuss the reactions they were experiencing and how these differed or were the same as those listed in the handout. In this group session the participants also learned from each other that they shared many similar feelings, including anger that safety measures and resources were being "poured into Manhattan, where the rich live, and not here where there is only us."

A very important part of the group process included the leader's ability to engage the participants in a discussion of coping strategies and mechanisms they had utilized to handle their responses to the disaster. Many of the women indicated that they were finding comfort in their religious beliefs and had been praying and attending church more often. Several said that coming to the support group had been helpful and pointed to this psychoeducational session as a specific example of that. Others found that talking to friends, listening to music, and walking had helped contain their anxiety. Several shared that they had been overeating to comfort themselves, which led to some joking and the observation that humor could also be helpful.

The social worker noted that three of the women in the group were experiencing significant distress beyond the expectable reactions. Ms. Martínez had been a victim and survivor of the war in El Salvador before migrating to the United States, where she thought she would be safe. The airplanes, fire, and rubble she saw on television reminded her of aerial military campaigns that had killed her father and brother. As a result, she was experiencing intrusive thoughts about their death and felt very frightened and unsafe. Another woman, Mrs. Gómez, had a son who had been murdered in Manhattan three years before. The media coverage of this part of the city and the loss of life as a result of the attacks were causing her to re experience her loss. Mrs. Molina, whose mother had passed away three years before on September 11, was experiencing an anniversary reaction (Gabriel, 1992). Consequently, any mention of September 11 or the events that transpired caused her to re experience the pain that was related to this earlier unresolved loss. Since all three of these women had prior traumatic experiences that significantly exacerbated their responses to the September 11 disaster, they were referred to a community mental health center with Spanish speaking social workers for ongoing individualized mental health services.

Following the psychoeducational session, the group was asked if they would like additional opportunities to discuss September 11. While the women felt that one session focused on the attacks had been sufficient at this time, the leader indicated that they could return to this topic, as needed, in the course of their ongoing group.

Discussion

This example illustrates differential responses to trauma and the importance of tailoring interventions according to individualized needs. Most of the women in the group were experiencing reactions that abated as a result of the knowledge gained and the mutual aid provided through the psychoeducational supportive group intervention. However, three of the women, because of pre existing vulnerable states, required a greater level of individualized intervention. The social worker served as a *consultant* to Ms. Ponce, *direct service provider (group worker)* and *educator* to the group, and a *broker* for the three women who were referred for additional services.

Summary

The practice examples presented in this chapter illustrate micro level generalist interventions with individuals, families, and groups in a diverse range of settings undertaken following the attacks on the World Trade Center. In all of these situations, generalist social workers carefully assessed needs and intervened accordingly in a variety of roles and at multiple levels. The next two chapters present examples of mezzo and macro level interventions in response to the events of September 11.

Chapter 6

Mezzo Level Generalist Practice:
Interventions within Agencies and Organizations

As discussed in Chapter 2, mezzo level interventions focus on organizational and agency change and development, in contrast to micro level interventions, which focus on work with individuals, families, and groups. For example, at the mezzo level, the social worker might facilitate organizational change to promote better service to clients and greater support of employees, coordinate service delivery among various agencies, and/or provide staff development and training.

This chapter discusses two types of mezzo level interventions that were provided to the staff of a large child welfare agency in the wake of the September 11 disaster. Administrators from the agency approached the faculty of a school of social work to request services for their employees, many who worked near the World Trade Center, had witnessed the collapse of the towers, and had been forced to flee their workplace. In addition to handling their reactions to the stress and trauma they experienced directly, the staff were responsible for the provision of services to children and families who, already under tremendous psychosocial stressors prior to September 11, were exhibiting increased behavioral and emotional difficulties.

The first mezzo level intervention that was provided was a series of psychoeducational support groups for agency staff. The second intervention, the need for which was uncovered through these groups, was the development and implementation of a training program for these staff to enable them to better understand, attend to, and support their ongoing work with clients in the context and aftermath of the World Trade Center attacks.

Agency wide Needs Assessment

When administrators from the child welfare agency requested services for potentially all of their hundreds of employees, the faculty of the school of social work relied on crisis intervention theories, practice principles and techniques, social work's person in environment perspective, and a generalist approach to address the realities and needs of this organization. In keeping with a crisis intervention perspective, the interventions were immediate, active, and focused on adaptation and coping. Likewise, since generalist practice principles prioritize the importance of starting where the client is and conducting a thorough assessment, a member of the social work faculty met with agency leaders to gather information about the organization's structure, purpose, and needs, in order to identify an appropriate intervention plan.

Groups are a common form of intervention in treating victims of trauma. There are two basic categories of groups used for this purpose: acute debriefing groups, which often are one time events and take place immediately following a disaster, and support groups which can take a variety of forms and often meet more than one time (Dembert & Simmer, 2000). Due to the large number of employees who witnessed the collapse of the towers, and the value of group interventions as a means to impart information, instill hope, and normalize experiences and feelings that may be experienced as unique (Yalom, 1995), a supportive and psychoeducational group format was selected as the intervention for this agency.

Given the widespread use and belief in the efficacy of group debriefing models for trauma victims (Armstrong et al., 1995; Bell, 1995; Chemtob, Thomas, Law, & Cremniter, 1997; Dembert & Simmer, 2000), before discussing the supportive psychoeducational group intervention used with this child welfare agency, we will discuss Critical Incident Stress Debriefing (CISD), a well known model of an acute debriefing group developed for use with rescue workers immediately following a crisis operation. Despite the extensive use of debriefing models, empirical research has raised questions about its effectiveness and has underscored the need for further research on the impact of this intervention (Bisson & Deahl, 1994; Boudreaux & McCabe, 2000; Gist & Woodall, 1998).

Critical Incident Stress Debriefing

As described by its developer, Mitchell (1983), the Critical Incident Stress Debriefing (CISD) model is a highly structured approach designed to manage the immediate stress response experienced by those exposed to a traumatic event and reduce the risk for more serious or delayed stress reactions. CISD consists of six segments, which can be provided in either an individual or group format. Mitchell describes the content of each of the six segments in the following way:

1. An introduction of the participants and facilitator, and a discussion about the group process and rules, such as confidentiality, that are to be followed

2. The fact phase, during which participants are asked to describe, in detail, their experiences of the incident

3. The facilitator encourages participants to discuss their feelings regarding the incident

4. The facilitator elicits information about unusual reactions, thoughts, or feelings participants might have experienced during the incident or in the aftermath

5. The facilitator provides education about the range of expectable physical, emotional, cognitive, psychological, and behavioral reactions to trauma. The purpose of steps three through five is to allow for ventilation of feelings as well as normalization and universalization of responses to a critical incident

6. The conclusion, which includes opportunities for the facilitator to answer questions, provide additional reassurance, help participants develop plans for the continued management of reactions, and make referrals to further resources, as needed

The CISD model requires between three to five hours, and may also include a follow up several weeks later. Variations of CISD have been widely used to debrief Red Cross personnel following various disasters (Armstrong, O'Callahan, & Marmar, 1991; Armstrong et al., 1995) and other victims or witnesses of trauma (Bell, 1995).

Challenges to Debriefing Approaches

As we have discussed, since evaluation is a crucial component of sound social work practice, all interventions should be studied in order to evaluate their efficacy. The research examining debriefing models is contradictory and inconclusive, clearly indicating the need for more rigorous study regarding its effectiveness and impact (Boudreaux & McCabe, 2000).

In several studies that have evaluated the perceived helpfulness of debriefing, participants have reported that the process is beneficial in reducing stress reactions (Burns & Harm, 1993). Other studies have found no significant differences in symptom levels between patients receiving debriefing and those receiving no intervention (Chemtob et al., 1997; Conlon, Fahy, & Conroy, 1998). However, a meta analysis of 10 controlled trials of debriefing indicates a beneficial outcome associated with debriefing (Everly, Boyle, & Lating, 1999). These researchers point out that one of the limitations of studies of debriefing has been a lack of uniformity and consistency in the definition and implementation of debriefing interventions. For example, in one study the debriefing intervention was a single, individual, 30 minute session, that focused on the expression of emotional and cognitive effects of an accident and provided education about posttraumatic stress symptoms, coping strategies, and referral information (Conlon et al., 1998). In another study, the debriefing intervention was a five hour group intervention, offered six months after a hurricane, which included three hours of group process and two hours of psychoeducation regarding stress reactions (Chemtob et al., 1997).

Of significant concern, some studies have described negative consequences resulting from debriefing. For example, a study examining the use of an individual, one hour, structured psychological debriefing intervention with victims of traffic accidents concluded that at four months post trauma, the intervention appeared to be ineffective, as indicated by the fact that victims continued to have substantial psychiatric symptoms (Hobbs, Mayou, & Harrison, 1996). In a three year follow up of this study, the researchers concluded that psychological debriefing was ineffective and had adverse long term effects. These conclusions were based on findings that indicated the intervention group had a "significantly worse outcome" and "patients who initially had high intrusion and avoidance symptoms remained symptomatic if they had received the intervention, but recovered if they did not receive the intervention" (Mayou, Ehlers, & Hobbs, 2000, p. 589).

These inconclusive and contradictory research findings underscore the need to further specify the definition of "debriefing" so that the efficacy of this intervention can be rigorously evaluated with specific populations and under particular circumstances. As we have described, generalist practice emphasizes the importance of ongoing evaluation of interventions, providing opportunities for social workers to take a leadership role in the initiation of research in this important area of practice.

Organizational Intervention:
The Provision of Psychoeducational Support Groups

In addition to debriefing groups, a second category of groups, psychoeducational support group interventions, are often used with victims of trauma (Dembert & Simmer, 2000). This is the type of intervention that was utilized by twelve social work faculty who conducted over forty groups, beginning six days after the disaster, at the large child welfare agency requesting assistance. The groups were provided for all levels of staff, including clerical, casework, supervisory, and managerial. Groups for line staff were held separately from those for supervisors and managers so that line staff participants would feel free to discuss all their concerns without fear of their supervisors' evaluation (Armstrong et al., 1995).

The groups were designed to identify and solve problems regarding issues and worries the staff had about the disaster as well as the transition back to their jobs. The groups utilized a structured problem solving psychoeducational format that stressed adaptation and coping and also allowed for continual assessment of individuals who might require additional interventions. Thus, the groups were designed to assess and promote both personal and professional functioning.

The facilitators of each group identified themselves as social workers who had been asked by agency leaders to speak with staff about their experiences and offer information about expectable reactions to trauma. At the outset of the groups, the facilitators outlined and explained the purpose of the groups, gave guidelines regarding confidentiality and respect for each other's views and experiences, and reviewed the structure and format of the session. The voluntary nature of the groups was stressed.

The facilitation of groups became an iterative process—as the groups unfolded, the facilitators discovered elements of the groups that worked or did not work, and also identified which components the participants found especially helpful. All of this information was used to focus and guide the facilitation of subsequent groups.

As generalist practitioners, the facilitators relied on the social work tenet of starting where the client is. Participants first wanted to talk about their experience of the disaster—where they were, what they saw, how they felt, what they did. Many of them had been at an office just blocks from the World Trade Center and had witnessed the planes crash into the towers and the subsequent collapse of the buildings. These staff participants reported that they had been trapped in the lobby of their building for some time. Moreover, when they were ordered to evacuate the building, the air outside was so thick with debris that they were unable to exit. Participants were able to observe and share reactions that were similar to those of their colleagues, which they found comforting.

The group process then moved naturally to a discussion of participants' reactions after the event. Participants reported feeling anxious, sad, and angry, and having difficulty concentrating, eating, and sleeping. The facilitators provided psychoeducation and distributed handouts about expectable behavioral, cognitive, emotional, physical, and psychological responses to trauma (see Chapter 4) as well as specific strategies to address and ameliorate these reactions.

Facilitators encouraged participants to share adaptive coping strategies that they found helpful. Group members reported strategies such as spending time with their families, attending religious services, exercising, cleaning, listening to music, and "keeping busy." Participants discussed the advantages and disadvantages of returning to the site of the World Trade towers. Some had returned to the site and found this helpful while others reported that they purposely avoided the site on their way to work, expressed considerable fear about going to the site, and vowed they would never return to it.

Participants reported that the most effective element of the group was the "mutual aid" that developed as a result of the leader's ability to elicit and use the participants' wide range of responses to the trauma and coping mechanisms to assist members in helping each other. In addition, the participants valued the opportunity to voice their concerns in a forum that was confidential. In this regard, it was particularly important that the leader was a neutral listener who was not connected to their workplace, and that there was an opportunity for ventilation with the knowledge that some general recommendations would be brought back to the management of the organization.

The facilitators assessed, in an on going way, participants who might require additional interventions or referrals, and when indicated, provided them with relevant referrals for individualized services. For example, one woman lived near an airport and was hiding under her bed every time she heard an airplane, which was quite frequently. She had not left her home except to come to work, and then only with great difficulty.

Given the impact her reactions were having on her daily functioning, she was referred for further services. Participants were also encouraged to attend additional groups at the agency, as needed, as several groups were being facilitated each day by this team of social workers.

Crisis as Opportunity

In addition to providing participants with a forum to process their reactions to the disaster itself, the groups crystallized and exposed many underlying problems within the organization. Recurrent themes raised in the groups often referred both to the participants' immediate concerns related to the disaster, as well as long standing systemic problems within the agency. Thus, the groups provided opportunities to identify and address organizational needs and to plan interventions aimed at organizational development and change. In this way, the micro level group service generated valuable information and feedback that could be used for mezzo level change to improve systemic and structural problems within the agency.

One overarching theme raised in the groups was safety. Participants, like many individuals in New York City and throughout the country, were worried about the immediate safety of themselves and their families. Specifically, they worried about the structural soundness and air quality of the work site, and were concerned about the lack of a disaster plan both at the time of the attacks and after. Since staff were asked to return to the building before it was adequately cleaned, many participants felt the agency was not concerned about their well being. Moreover, other buildings in the vicinity of the World Trade Center had already been extensively cleaned, causing participants to feel further neglected by the organization's administration.

A second pervasive theme that emerged in the groups was the difficulty staff were experiencing in returning to their jobs. This was due, in part, to the expectable and normative problems participants had concentrating on their work because of overwhelming fears and desires to be at home with their children and families. There were also realistic obstacles that resulted from the fact that the telephone and computer lines were down and had not yet been replaced.

These common themes led to discussions about the difficulties and frustrations workers experienced in their everyday work lives. Each day, staff confronted complex and disturbing issues related to the neglect, abuse, and, occasionally, the death of children. They were expected to carry huge caseloads but were offered few resources to help them function effectively in their jobs. The group participants expressed considerable dissatisfaction with the organization regarding these issues. While anger is a predictable response to trauma (Taffel, 2001), staff clearly expressed pervasive feelings of frustration and discontent related to longstanding problems they experienced with the existing structure and policies of the agency.

In one of the managers' groups, participants developed a set of recommendations for the organization designed to address some of these concerns that included the following suggestions:

- Development of an overall disaster plan for the building, including the development of a method of contacting staff in the event of another emergency, including a "phone chain" or through the use of newspapers, radio, and television

- Provision of additional security in the building

- Washing all the windows in the building, which were still covered with soot and ashes

- Provision of gas masks to staff who wanted them

- Provision of on site counseling, as needed, for staff

- Public acknowledgement and closure on the part of the organization regarding the trauma in the form of a structured ritual

- De emphasis of statistics and productivity levels during the transition period immediately following the disaster

- Ongoing training in risk management and disaster preparedness

All staff members were encouraged to voice to their supervisors concerns and suggestions regarding recommendations for overall organizational improvement, in addition to suggestions resulting from September 11. The group facilitators gleaned and synthesized salient findings from the various groups, drafted a memo, and met with agency leaders to convey these concerns in the form of recommendations for review by management in areas such as workload assignment, additional support services for staff, and improved communication between staff and management.

Agency wide Training Program

One significant organizational level need uncovered as a result of this process was the need to train staff more fully regarding the impact of trauma on themselves and their clients. It was evident that in addition to the trauma resulting from September 11, the staff also encountered trauma daily in their very difficult and challenging jobs, placing them at risk for vicarious traumatization. Vicarious traumatization, as the term suggests, refers to the distressing behavioral, cognitive, emotional, physical, and psychological reactions a helper can experience as a result of listening to and helping individuals who have experienced trauma (O'Halloran & Linton, 2000; McCann & Pearlman, 1999; Ryan, 1999; Sexton, 1999). This phenomenon, also known as secondary traumatic stress or "compassion fatigue", is being studied in order to develop techniques for its management and prevention (Sexton, 1999).

The development of an agency wide training program is the second example of a mezzo level intervention undertaken within this organization. As a result of the assessment process described, it was felt that training and education regarding reactions to trauma would help staff members work more effectively with their clients—children, parents, and foster parents. Moreover, additional training could also provide education to them about their own reactions to trauma and reduce the risk of vicarious traumatization.

A team of representatives from nearly forty child welfare agencies, advocacy groups and foundations met to create a curriculum for child welfare clients and staff. The goals of the training were for clients and staff to learn about the range of immediate and short term responses to the September 11 attacks as well as the impact of other kinds of trauma. A three hour training module was developed for child welfare line staff. This module included the following topics:

1. The definition of traumatic stress, including risk factors for its development

2. Normative, age specific responses to trauma, loss, and disaster

3. Education regarding issues specific to the child welfare field, including the pre existing vulnerabilities of grief and loss in this population, the impact of disaster on outcomes such as placements and permanency planning, and the impact of disaster on the system itself, in the form of increased referrals and staff stress

4. Coping strategies adults can utilize to help children, supervisors can use to help workers, and agencies can employ to support their staff

5. Vicarious traumatization in staff, including strategies to identify and address this syndrome with staff

6. Problematic stress responses and how to access resources and referrals

The training modules were refined and made relevant for each of the various populations that staff encountered in their work, including foster parents, birth parents, daycare staff, managers, and mental health professionals. In keeping with the important principle of assessing and examining practice, the training program will be pilot tested before it is implemented. Once implemented, the training program will be evaluated for its relevance and effectiveness with each of the specified populations.

Discussion

The two examples presented in this chapter are excellent illustrations of generalist practice. Psychoeducational group services for staff were conceptualized from a mezzo level perspective to address the needs of an agency. The evaluation of these group interventions led to the identification of structural problems within the organization, as well as the need for training to better serve both agency staff and their clients. Through a mezzo level intervention, the agency leaders were informed of workers' concerns and were engaged in the planning, development and implementation of the training module.

During the course of the two mezzo level interventions that were undertaken in this agency in response to the September 11 World Trade Center attack, generalist practitioners assumed a variety of roles. In meeting with the child welfare agency leaders, assessing the needs of agency staff, creating and implementing the supportive psychoeducational group interventions, and conveying feedback to management in order to foster change, the social workers played the roles of *group work service providers, program developers, educators,* and *advocates.* In addition, they assumed the roles of *organizational change agents* to help staff make their views known to management, and *brokers* when referring individuals for additional services. By identifying the need for training, organizing and hosting the meeting of various agency representatives, and overseeing the development, implementation, and evaluation of a training curriculum on trauma, social workers assumed the roles of *program planners/developers, facilitators, educators/trainers, consultants* to the agency and *researchers.*

Summary

In Chapter 5 we discussed practice illustrations of micro level interventions provided to individuals, families, and groups in the wake of September 11. This chapter has discussed two mezzo level interventions that were provided to staff within a large public child welfare agency. The first of these interventions, psychoeducational staff support groups, led to the second intervention, the development and implementation of an agency wide training program. The next chapter discusses macro level interventions conducted in the New York City community in response to September 11.

Chapter 7

Macro Level Generalist Practice: Planning, Coordination, and Delivery of Crisis Intervention and Disaster Services

Thus far we have discussed micro and mezzo level practice in which generalist practitioners provide direct interventions to systems of all sizes, including individuals, families, groups, and organizations. This chapter considers macro level practice, which shifts the focus of intervention from the provision of *direct* services to *indirect* services. Indirect services are concerned with the overall ways in which social services are planned, organized, implemented, administered, and delivered, and social welfare policies are developed, analyzed, and formulated.

As is the case in micro and mezzo levels of intervention, the macro level practitioner engages in the five stages of practice that were described in Chapter 2: engagement, assessment, planning, implementation, and evaluation of interventions. Macro level interventions require that the generalist practitioner target change efforts at larger systems such as the community, city, state, and nation.

As described in Chapter 1, September 11 was, in the words of Tucker et al., "a complex disaster with many layers of physical and emotional exposure" (1999, p. 78). There are the victims and survivors as well as their families, loved ones, friends, and colleagues. There are those who lost their homes, businesses, or jobs. There are the rescue workers, helpers, and clean up crews, at risk for vicarious traumatization. The extensive and continuous media coverage created a "larger global disaster community" across the country and, indeed, the world (Tucker et al., 1999, p. 78). In a similar way, Golan (1978) describes those affected by a disaster as the "community of sufferers" (p. 126) who experience both individual and collective distress and suffering.

These authors point out that tragedy and disaster do not have clearly defined boundaries nor are the effects of disaster limited to the immediate area of destruction. Others (Wright et al., 1990) have noted that "the consequences [of traumatic events] can reach across nations and oceans, requiring a broadened perspective for the identification of those at risk following disaster" (p. 37). It is this broadened perspective which has been promoted in this book.

In keeping with this expanded definition, the disaster community created as a result of September 11 clearly extended far beyond the areas of New York and Arlington, Virginia, where the attacks occurred, and rural Pennsylvania, where a plane crashed. The disaster community grew to include the victims, survivors, and their loved ones in these areas, as well as many individuals across the nation and around the world. This conceptualization of those potentially affected by disaster requires a macro level approach to the planning, development and implementation of multiple programs and services to meet the needs of this wide range of people, organizations, and institutions.

This chapter describes three macro level examples of the planning, organization, development, implementation, and delivery of services in New York to meet city and statewide needs in response to the disaster of September 11. The first example concerns the delivery of comprehensive services organized immediately following the attacks for those most directly affected by the disaster—family members and loved ones of individuals who were lost, as well as those individuals who witnessed and survived the disaster. The second example discusses *Project Liberty*, a program that provides services throughout New York City and state for all individuals who were affected by the disaster. The final example describes the efforts of the New York City chapter of the National Association of Social Workers, a national professional organization, to reach out to social work practitioners throughout New York City in order to assess needs, and to organize, coordinate, and plan future services.

These illustrations highlight principles of generalist practice that have been discussed throughout this book: the assumption of multiple social work roles, the implementation of a wide range of skills at each stage in the intervention process, and intervention at micro, mezzo and macro levels.

Comprehensive Service Delivery to Individuals and Families: The Family Assistance Center

During the week following September 11, the Mayor's Office of Community Affairs, in coordination with the New York City Police Department, set up a comprehensive service center referred to as the Family Assistance Center. The Family Assistance Center was located at a large public armory to serve as a central location for the provision of a wide range of crisis intervention and concrete services to individuals and family members impacted by the disaster. Social service and mental health staff from the city and state Departments of Mental Health, personnel from a variety of local, state and federal agencies, and voluntary organizations such as The Red Cross and the Salvation Army, were available to assist individuals and family members who presented with multiple concrete, emotional, and psychological needs.

Services available at the Family Assistance Center included: crisis intervention, supportive counseling, and bereavement services provided by clergy and mental health professionals; psychiatric evaluations provided by disaster psychiatry services; law enforcement stations to report missing persons; information on hospitalized individuals; DNA testing to aid in the identification of relatives; the issuance of death certificates; legal services; immigration services; financial entitlements provided by the Crime Victims Board for immediate needs such as food, clothing, and personal items; and other concrete services, such as services related to relocation and housing. In addition, there were services designed specifically for children in a "Kids' Corner".

After its first week of operation, The Family Assistance Center was relocated to a large pier in order to provide additional space to accommodate others impacted by the attacks on the World Trade Center, such as those who were displaced from or lost their jobs. New services that were incorporated included job placement, vocational training, health benefits provision, and support to businesses impacted by the disaster.

One of the important services provided at the Family Assistance Center were daily boat rides to bring bereaved family members and friends to the site of the World Trade Center and a Memorial Park set up for grieving family members and friends. Several mental health professionals were available on each boat to support family members in this extremely difficult and emotional experience. This service required a high level of comfort, skill, and flexibility on the part of the practitioner in order to be available to family members in whatever ways they needed. Individuals and families, depending on socioeconomic, cultural, ethnic, and religious differences, had a wide range of responses to the tragedy and loss resulting from the disaster. Accordingly, generalist practitioners responded with a wide range of concrete and supportive interventions consistent with the varied ways in which the family members mourned.

The organization of all the services in one location reflected core principles of generalist practice discussed in Chapter 2: "staring where the client is" and conceptualizing needs from a person in environment perspective. The following example from the Family Assistance Center illustrates how the integration of concrete and counseling services in one location allowed social workers to identify and assess needs that existed beyond the concerns with which individuals initially presented.

Ms. Pérez

Ms. Pérez is a 33 year old Puerto Rican woman who came to the Family Assistance Center seeking help with the payment of her rent. She was referred to a benefits worker, who began asking Ms. Pérez questions about her financial situation. At this point, Ms. Pérez became distressed and tears came to her eyes. She explained to the benefits worker that she was not seeking financial assistance. Rather, she was unable to write a check to her landlord because she had forgotten her landlord's name. She was worried she would be evicted because her rent was due on the 15th of each month, and it was already September 21. The benefits worker called for a social worker to meet with Ms. Pérez.

After introducing herself, the social worker noted the rather sudden change in Ms. Pérez's affect and gently inquired about where she had been at the time of the disaster. Ms. Pérez replied that she worked as a security guard in Tower One and had been at her post patrolling the lobby at the time that the building had been hit. She then recounted her actions in great detail, which she stated she was able to do, as she could not stop thinking about and reliving the moments after the impact.

As she had been trained to do, Ms. Pérez helped evacuate people from the building following the crash. She was escorting a woman whose clothes had been burnt off outside to a waiting ambulance when she heard loud noises, saw people jumping from above, and then realized that the noises were bodies landing beside her. Within minutes, the second tower was hit and Ms. Pérez could not recall her escape further. For the past ten days, Ms. Pérez had been unable to sleep, experienced nightmares, was hypervigilant, believed that someone was following her, and was re experiencing the moments after the impact, but having difficulty remembering most of what had occurred to her and others on and after September 11. These are all symptoms of Post Traumatic Stress Disorder (see Chapter 4).

The social worker discussed with Ms. Pérez that her symptoms were expectable given the extent of her exposure to the trauma, and encouraged her to get some help and support in dealing with them. Ms. Pérez stated that she would prefer meeting with someone who could speak Spanish. The social worker inquired where Ms. Pérez lived, and was able to locate a community mental health center with a Spanish speaking social worker in her neighborhood. The social worker called the agency so that Ms. Pérez was able to speak directly to the staff and make an appointment for the following day. The social worker also was able to use city records to find out the landlord's name so that Ms. Pérez could remit her rent.

Discussion

Conceptualized from a generalist perspective, the Family Assistance Center provided comprehensive micro level services planned from a macro level perspective to address multiple needs, and to maximize the access, efficiency, and effectiveness of delivery. The diverse scope of services provided to individuals and families at the Family Assistance Center reflected the wide range of urgent physical, emotional, psychological, familial, and concrete needs that arose in the hours, days, and weeks immediately following the disaster. Reflecting a generalist approach to practice, social workers who helped establish the Family Assistance Center assumed multiple roles as *service planners*, *organizers*, and *developers*. Moreover, the social workers who provided services at the Family Assistance Center assumed roles as *counselors*, *advocates*, *case managers,* and *brokers* of services. On both levels, in the establishment of the Center and in the provision of services at the Center, generalist practitioners used their wide repertoire of skills to differentially address all levels of need. Thus, individuals and families could simultaneously obtain a range of concrete services and resources and/or crisis intervention and emotional support services.

In the case of Ms. Pérez, the social worker possessed a wide repertoire of generalist skills in *engagement*, *assessment*, *crisis intervention*, *counseling*, *case management*, and linkage to more comprehensive, individualized services. Moreover, the model of service delivery at the center incorporated both concrete and counseling services in an accessible and comprehensive manner which reflects the principles of crisis intervention and generalist practice that have been discussed throughout this book.

Project Liberty

Project Liberty is a crisis counseling program, federally funded through the Federal Emergency and Management Agency (FEMA), that was developed in response to the September 11 disaster. The program provides free crisis counseling services including outreach, individual, group, and family crisis counseling, and public education to anyone throughout the state of New York who was affected by the September 11 disaster. In collaboration with the New York State Office of Mental Health, the program is locally administered by the New York City Department of Mental Health as well as the ten surrounding counties that were included in the Presidential disaster declaration (http://www.projectliberty.state.ny.us/).

Project Liberty utilizes the slogan "Feel Free to Feel Better" to advertise services on subways and buses in response to the disaster of September 11. The advertisements, written in both English and Spanish, also include statements such as "We're all in this together. But if you're feeling alone, call us," as well as comments from individuals regarding their feelings about the attacks and their coping strategies. For example, one man wrote: "I guess what I'm doing to cope is to play pick up ball in the neighborhood park, cook for my girlfriend, attend more 12 step meetings so I don't relapse, find other support, and check in with my friends often" (Project Liberty advertisement, 2001).

Project Liberty was conceptualized, developed, and designed in a manner consistent with a generalist social work practice perspective, incorporating key principles of this approach that have been discussed throughout this book. These include: the wide variety of generalist social work roles; the blending of concrete with counseling services; and the multiple levels of intervention—micro, mezzo, and macro—at which generalist practitioners provide services.

As illustrated in the following excerpts from Project Liberty brochures, both concrete and counseling services aimed at prevention and early intervention were offered in a wide range of settings to all those affected by the September 11 disaster:

> Project Liberty counselors are trained to talk with you about your concerns. They will help you consider how best to meet your needs and suggest options. They will also help you with other resources you may need. If you would like to find a grief support group in your neighborhood, for example, we will help you do this.

Other services provided by Project Liberty include:

- Meeting with a small group of relatives to hear how they have been feeling since the disaster, to help them understand their responses, and to think of ways they can support each other in handling them

- Leading a discussion of a church group to help group members become aware of normal reactions to a disaster, how to avoid long term problems, and where to get more help, when needed

- Training teachers and aides to know signs that school children may show when they have trouble coping

- Talking with a group of employees during a brown bag lunch about normal responses and healthy ways to cope with trauma

- Leading a discussion of a mother's group, to help the mothers understand a toddler's normal reactions to a disaster and ways to help them cope

- Training the health staff of a large financial firm to help employees recognize signs that may indicate trouble coping with the disaster and what to do (http://www.projectliberty.state.ny.us/; New York State Office of Mental Health, 2001)

Discussion

Several key concepts of generalist and crisis theory are evident in Project Liberty's advertising campaign. First, the ads imply that many people were affected by the disaster, that a range of reactions are normal, and that people can often benefit from support provided by others. Second, the services are available to all, and the location of services is based on the needs of the individuals, families, groups, organizations, and/or communities that are requesting services. As indicated in the brochures promoting Project Liberty (2001), services can be provided "anywhere, including homes, businesses, schools, colleges, houses of worship, shelters, and community centers. You can have services scheduled at a time that best meets your personal or group needs." This aspect of the program reflects the importance of outreach (see Chapter 5), a key element of crisis theory and practice, and a way to provide services to those in need within their natural environments.

NASW Survey

Several months after the disaster, the New York City Chapter of the National Association of Social Workers sent a survey to its membership requesting information on the volunteer efforts they provided in response to the World Trade Center attacks, the plane crash in Far Rockaway, New York, and/or the anthrax threat. The collection of this type of information for the purposes of research, planning, and program development is another example of macro level practice.

The survey sought information concerning the ways in which social workers were involved in these disasters. Specifically, information was sought regarding the type and length of social work services that were provided. Such data is helpful in documenting the contributions of the social work profession and in identifying ways that social workers can respond to future disasters. The survey also sought information about any obstacles social workers encountered in the provision of services. This feedback is crucial for evaluation of change in existing programs and for the planning and development of new services to assist in disaster situations.

The survey also represented an effort to develop a database of volunteers who were willing to offer additional services over the next months. In order to match potential need with available services, the survey requested information about the skills, language capability, and availability of these social workers. The organization and accessibility of information about existing skills, resources, and needs is essential in planning for effective and efficient service delivery. Moreover, this information is also critical for planning and developing future services, including efforts at prevention and early intervention.

Additionally, the survey requested that respondents describe the types of services, such as training, support groups, and debriefings, that they would like to receive from the National Association of Social Workers. Thus, it served as an assessment of training needs and supports that social workers in the field require in order to effectively respond to a disaster such as occurred on September 11, and will likely spur the development of such services.

Discussion

This survey is a good example of macro level generalist intervention because it gathered information relevant for program change, planning and development. In addition, it constituted a beginning effort at researching and evaluating social work interventions in response to a disaster, which will be useful in preparing social workers to respond to future crisis situations.

Summary

This chapter provided three examples of macro level practice in the aftermath of September 11. The fundamental principles of generalist social work practice discussed throughout this book—the person in environment perspective, intervention at various levels, integration of practice, policy and research, careful assessment, and the assumption of multiple roles—are evident in the planning, development and implementation of these programs and services.

PART IV

CONCLUSION

Chapter 8

Lessons Learned and Future Directions for Social Work Practice, Policy, Education, Training, and Research

By linking the theory, knowledge, skills, and values of generalist practice and crisis intervention, this book has established a conceptual framework to guide social workers in response to disaster. This framework for practice has been illustrated through examples of actual interventions undertaken by social workers with a variety of client systems in the aftermath of September 11.

As discussed throughout this book, the series of events that transpired on September 11 and the emotional, physical, psychological, economic, social, cultural and spiritual reverberations have left an impact on a great many people. As Golan (1978) suggests, the "community of sufferers" created by these events comprises individuals of wide ranging age, class, ethnic group composition, socioeconomic strata, and geographic location. During the events of September 11 and in its aftermath, social workers assumed, and will continue to assume, important and varied roles attending to the diverse populations of individuals, families, groups, organizations, and communities differentially affected by this disaster.

While most of the vignettes presented in this book illustrate social work practice that was provided in the days, weeks, and months immediately following the attacks, we have also underscored the importance of viewing the events surrounding September 11 from a long term perspective. Given the widespread reverberations of the attacks, coupled with the ever present possibility of future disaster, we conclude this book by reviewing some of the lessons we have learned from these tragic events. Finally, in looking forward to the future, beyond September 11, we discuss the implications of these lessons for the social work profession, and provide some initial suggestions for social work practice and policy, education and training, and research in situations of disaster. In addition, while much has been learned about responding to disaster, there remain many gaps in our understanding of this area of practice. Thus, we provide a section on select resources for further learning at the end of the chapter.

As we have underscored throughout this book, since there are intrinsic interrelationships between the areas of social work practice, policy, and research, there will be overlap and connections in the discussion of these areas in this chapter.

Practice and Policy

A generalist approach to social work practice provides a highly relevant framework for social work intervention in situations of disaster because it is an approach that addresses all systems and levels of intervention, integrates practice, policy, and research, and is based on the fundamental social work tenet of "starting where the client is." Crisis intervention is an equally essential practice approach in disaster situations because of its immediate, active, and directive focus on restoring client systems to their previous level of functioning by capitalizing on the heightened motivation, capacity, and opportunity engendered by crisis.

Throughout this book, we have emphasized the multiple roles generalist social workers assumed during the September 11 disaster. These varied roles as advocate, broker, clinician, community organizer, educator, group worker, organizational analyst and change agent, planner, program developer, and trainer, combine diverse social work functions including assessment, counseling, crisis intervention, prevention, and service delivery.

As we have learned from our experience following the attacks of September 11, as well as from research studies of other disaster situations, social workers need to be capable of responding in an immediate and efficient manner to large numbers of individuals who present a broad range of needs (Soliman & Rogge, 2002; Tucker et al., 1999; Wright et al., 1990). Moreover, it is critical that social workers focus particular attention on vulnerable populations such as children or the disabled, as well as populations who are already disenfranchised, marginalized, or at risk.

As conveyed by the practice vignettes presented, some of the individuals who experienced significant emotional and psychological reactions to the disaster were reluctant to seek services because they did not want to think of themselves as "emotionally disturbed." As Taffel (2001) points out, "despite the enormity of what had happened, it was still a major stigma to be seen as needy or weak" (p. 24). Therefore, as discussed in Chapter 5, community based outreach services were important because they provided a useful model of service delivery in the aftermath of September 11 that destigmatized and normalized peoples' responses to the disaster and emphasized the importance of seeking assistance and support. Such a model should be examined as a way of providing services in the future.

In diverse settings, including hospitals, schools, agencies, and places of employment, models of group work, such as those discussed in Chapters 5 and 6, offered participants valuable opportunities for education, intervention, problem solving, prevention, and support. As discussed in Chapter 6, many of the groups conducted in the aftermath of September 11 combined elements of the Critical Incident Stress Debriefing (CISD) model which have not yet been fully studied and evaluated. This is an important opportunity for social workers to build on the successful elements of group models that utilize strategies such as psychoeducation and debriefing, and simultaneously evaluate the efficacy of these groups, in order to develop models that will be effective in the future.

Before September 11, it was not possible to foresee or be prepared for such an event. The reality of this experience forces us as individuals, and as a profession, to be prepared, as best as is possible, for potential disasters in the future. Social policy must incorporate key aspects of learning from this experience, particularly developing, planning, funding, and institutionalizing service delivery systems for those affected by disaster. Such systems need to be universally accessible, efficient, and provide services and resources with a minimum of paperwork and delay.

An important area of learning beyond September 11 is the service delivery model of the Family Assistance Center, which provided services in a universally accessible, expedient, one stop shopping approach. This model should be considered as a possible template for an efficient and effective way to routinely offer services and benefits to those requiring assistance—not only in times of disaster.

Education and Training

The capacity to respond to multiple client systems with varying needs through the assumption of a variety of roles requires the training of social work students as well as experienced practitioners capable of responding immediately in broad, flexible ways, within a generalist practice model. These social service providers must be trained in attending to the normal expectable responses to trauma, and in crisis intervention. To meet these needs, schools of social work, agencies, and professional organizations will need to integrate rigorous training regarding these practice domains into their educational programs.

Many mental health professionals and social service providers attempted to volunteer in the aftermath of the September 11 attacks. However, given the enormity of the disaster, the unprecedented number of volunteers, and the exceptional range of needs presented, it was difficult to coordinate these volunteer services. Moreover, not all volunteers were trained or skilled to handle crisis and disaster. To be better prepared for future disaster, it is important that schools of social work, as well as continuing education programs in social work practice settings, provide specific training for the multiple generalist practice roles that are required for intervention and prevention in handling situations of crisis and disaster. It will then be possible to have a large pool of appropriately trained social workers organized and available for deployment in an expedient manner should the need arise.

There are high levels of stress and responsibility placed on those who provide services in response to disaster. The enormous needs generated by September 11 prompted social workers to continue the development of effective methods to provide "help for the helpers." Social work, mental health, and other professional staff who provided services in the aftermath of the September 11 disaster required frequent opportunities to process, "debrief," and obtain support for themselves, to assure that they could effectively help others. For example, at the Family Assistance Center, all service providers—whether lawyers helping family members with legal paperwork, social workers assisting survivors, or child care workers volunteering at the Kids' Corner—were strongly encouraged to participate in at least one support group each day to debrief and obtain necessary and ongoing support. Similarly, mental health professionals who assisted bereaved family members at the World Trade Center site or at the morgue also required intensive debriefing and support. Ways of preventing and managing the phenomenon of vicarious traumatization will need to be further researched in an effort to attend to social workers in their everyday work roles and to prepare for future disasters.

Research

The attacks of September 11, and our response to these events, have underscored the need for further research in multiple areas. It is essential to learn more about successful and effective interventions, as well as to better understand the short and long term needs of individuals affected by disaster, particularly the bereaved family members of those lost, the survivors and their families, and all vulnerable populations. Research is also warranted to examine effective ways of providing "help for the helpers" through prevention and management of vicarious traumatization. Moreover, what can be done from a practice, policy, training, and research perspective to be better prepared in the future? Answers to such questions will significantly improve our ability to intervene appropriately and expediently. Some further questions to examine include:

1. What can we learn from survivors about their needs, coping strategies, and what interventions would be helpful to them?

2. What can we learn from bereaved family members and loved ones about their needs, coping strategies, and what interventions would be helpful to them?

3. What can we learn from specific populations such as children, frail elderly, people of color, and people with disabilities, about their needs following disaster and what interventions would be helpful to them?

4. What will be the long term effects for survivors and how will they fare? What supports can be put into place?

5. What will be the long term effects for the bereaved and how will they fare? What supports can be put into place?

6. Which interventions, programs, and policies instituted following September 11 proved to be useful? In what ways? What might they teach us about preparedness for future disasters?

7. How can these interventions, programs and policies be evaluated?

8. Who develops Post Traumatic Stress Disorder and what interventions are useful in its treatment and prevention?

9. Is debriefing a helpful intervention? If so, what kind of training is needed for its appropriate use?

Summary

Social workers played active and vital roles in responding to September 11 because they possess the values, knowledge base, and skills necessary to attend to the diverse needs presented by the multiple client systems that were impacted by this disaster. The melding of generalist practice and crisis intervention presented in this book can support social workers in these functions.

We have learned a great deal about intervention in situations of disaster through these tragic events. Of equal importance, we have uncovered many gaps in our understanding and knowledge which will need to be filled in order for us to continue attending to the needs arising in the wake of this disaster, and to be better prepared for other disasters that may occur beyond September 11.

The final section of this chapter presents select resources for further learning. Intervention in disaster situations requires special understanding, knowledge, and skills, and we look forward to change and development in these areas of social work. Such growth will more adequately prepare us as individuals, and as a profession, to better respond in the wake of disaster.

Resources for Further Learning

Aguilera, D., & Messick, J. (1990). *Crisis intervention theory and methodology*. St. Louis, MI: C. V. Mosby.

Charney, A. E., & Pearlman, L. A. (1998). The ecstasy and the agony: The impact of disaster and trauma work on the self of the clinician. In P. Kleepsies (Ed.), *Emergencies in mental health practice: Evaluation and management*, (pp. 418 435). New York: The Guilford Press.

Cherry, A., & Cherry, M. (1997). A middle class response to disaster: FEMA's policies and problems. *Journal of Social Service Research, 23* (1), 71 87.

Cosgrove, J. G. (2000). Social workers in disaster mental health services: The American Red Cross. *Tulane Studies in Social Welfare, 21 22*, 117 128.

Cowger, D. C. (1994). Assessing client strengths: Clinical assessment for client empowerment. *Social Work, 39* (3), 262 269.

Delgado, M. (2000). *Community social work practice in an urban context: The potential of a capacity enhancement perspective.* New York: Oxford University Press.

DeVries, M. W., & Hobfoil, S. (Eds.). (1995). *Extreme stress and communities*. Boston: Kluwer Academic Publishers.

Dingman, R. L., & Ginter, E. J. (1995). Disasters and crises: The role of mental health counseling. *Journal of Mental Health Counseling, 17* (3), 259 263.

Dodds, S., & Nuehring, E. (1996). A primer for social work research on disaster. In C. L. Streeter & S. A. Murty (Eds.). *Research on social work and disasters*, (pp. 27 56). New York: Haworth.

Eranen, L., & Liebkind, K. (1993). Coping with disaster: The helping behavior of communities and individuals. In J. P. Wilson & B. Raphael (Eds.), *International handbook of traumatic stress syndromes*, (pp. 957 964). New York: Plenum Press.

Fauri, D. P., Wernet, S. P., & Netting, F. E. (Eds.). (2000). *Cases in macro social work practice*. Boston: Allyn and Bacon.

Figley, C. R. (Ed.). (1995). *Compassion fatigue: Coping with secondary traumatic stress disorder in those who treat the traumatized*. New York: Brunner/Mazel.

Fothergill, A., Maestas, E. G., & Darlington, J. D. (1999). Race, ethnicity and disasters in the United States: A review of the literature. *Disasters, 23* (2), 156 173.

Freud, S. (1936). *The ego and the mechanisms of defense*. New York: International Universities Press.

Gabriel, M. (1992). Anniversary reactions: Trauma revisited. *Clinical Social Work Journal, 20* (2), 179 192.

Germain, C. B. (1991). *Human behavior in the social environment: An ecological view*. New York: Columbia University Press.

Gillespie, D. F., & Murty, S. A. (1994). Cracks in a post disaster service delivery network. *American Journal of Community Psychology, 22,* 639 660.

Ginexi, E. M., Weihs, K., Simmens, S. J., & Hoyt, D. R. (2000). Natural disaster and depression: A prospective investigation of reactions to the 1993 Midwest floods. *American Journal of Community Psychology, 28*, 495 518.

Goenjian, A. K., Molina, L., Steinberg, A. M., Fairbanks, L. A., Alvarez, M., Goenjian, H. A., & Pynoos, R. S. (2001). Posttraumatic stress and depressive reactions among Nicaraguan adolescents after Hurricane Mitch. *American Journal of Psychiatry, 158*, 788 794.

Goldstein, E. G., & Noonan, M. (1999). *Short term treatment and social work practice: An integrative perspective.* New York: The Free Press.

Green, B., Grace, M., Lindy, J., Gleser, G. C., Leonard, A. C., & Kramer, T. L. (1990). Buffalo Creek survivors in the second decade: Comparison with unexposed and nonlitigant groups. *Journal of Applied Social Psychology, 20*, 1033 50.

Gutiérrez, L. M. (1994). Beyond coping: An empowerment perspective on stressful life events. *Journal of Sociology and Social Welfare, 21* (3), 201 219.

Hanson, R. F., Kilpatrick, D. G., Freedy, J. R., & Saunders, B. E. (1995). Los Angeles County after the 1992 civil disturbances: Degree of exposure and impact on mental health. *Journal of Consulting and Clinical Psychology, 63*, 987 996.

Hartmann, H. (1939). *Ego psychology and the problem of adaptation.* New York: International Universities Press.

Horowitz, M. J. (Ed.). (1999). *Essential papers on posttraumatic stress disorder.* New York: New York University Press.

Horowitz, M. J. (2001). *Stress response syndromes.* Northvale, NJ: Jason Aronson.

James, R. K., & Gilliland, B. E. (2001). *Crisis intervention strategies*, (4th ed.). Belmont, CA: Brooks/Cole.

Jaswal, S. (2000). Disasters and mental health. *Indian Journal of Social Work, 61* (4), 521 526.

Kaniasty, K., & Norris, F. H. (1995). In search of altruistic community: Patterns of social support mobilization following Hurricane Hugo. *American Journal of Community Psychology, 23*, 447.

Kenardy, J. (2000). The current status of psychological debriefing. *British Medical Journal, 321*, 1032 1033.

Keranci, N. A., & Aksit, B. (2000). Building disaster resistant communities: Lessons learned from past earthquakes in Turkey and suggestions for the future. *International Journal of Mass Emergencies and Disasters, 18* (3), 403 416.

Kirst Ashman, K. K., & Straussner, S. L. A. (2002). *Generalist practice with organizations and communities*, (2nd ed.). Belmont, CA: Brooks/Cole.

Kruger, A. (2000). Empowerment in social work practice with the psychiatrically disabled: Model and method. *Smith College Studies in Social Work, 70* (3), 427 439.

Longres, J. F. (2000). *Human behavior in the social environment*, (3rd ed.). Itsaca, IL: F. E. Peacock Publishers, Inc.

Malkinson, R., Rubin, S. S., & Witzum, E. (Eds.). (2000). *Traumatic and nontraumatic loss and bereavement: Clinical theory and practice*. Madison, CT: Psychosocial Press.

McFarlane, A. (1990). Post traumatic stress syndrome revisited. In H. Parad & L. Parad (Eds.), *Crisis intervention book 2: The practitioner's source book for brief therapy.* Milwaukee, WI: Family Service America.

McMillen, J. C., Smith, E. M., & Fisher, R. H. (1997). Perceived benefit and mental health after three types of disaster. *Journal of Consulting and Clinical Psychology, 65,* 733 739.

McMillen, J. C. (1999). Better for it: How people benefit from adversity. *Social Work, 44,* 455 467.

McQuaide, S., & Ehrenreich, J. H. (1997). Assessing client strengths. *Families in Society, 78* (2), 201 212.

Meenaghan, T. M., & Gibbons, W. E. (2000). *Generalist practice in larger settings.* Chicago: Lyceum Books, Inc.

North, C. S., & Hong, B. A. (2000). Project CREST: A new model for mental health intervention after a community disaster. *American Journal of Public Health, 90,* 1057 58.

Norwood, A. E., Ursano, R. J., & Fullerton, C. S. (2000). Disaster psychiatry: Principles and practice. *Psychiatric Quarterly, 71,* 207 226.

Ortega, A. N., & Rosenheck, R. (2000). Posttraumatic stress disorder among Hispanic Vietnam veterans. *American Journal of Psychiatry, 157,* 615 619.

Phillips, N. K., & Straussner, S. L. A. (2002). *Urban social work: An introduction to policy and practice in the cities.* Boston: Allyn and Bacon.

Regehr, C., & Hill, J. (2000). Evaluating the efficacy of crisis debriefing groups. *Social Work with Groups, 23,* 69 79.

Richman, N. (1997). Ethical issues in disaster and other extreme situations. In D. Black, M. Newman, J. Haris Hendriks & C. Mezey (Eds.). *Psychological trauma: A developmental approach.* London: Gaskell/Royal College of Psychiatrists.

Roberts, A. R. (Ed.). (1990). *Crisis intervention handbook: Assessment, treatment and research.* Belmont, CA: Wadsworth.

Ruef, A. M., Litz, B. T., & Schlenger, W. E. (2000). Hispanic ethnicity and risk for combat related posttraumatic stress disorder. *Cultural Diversity and Ethnic Minority Psychology, 6,* 235 251.

Shalev, A. Y., Freedman, S., Peri, T., Brandes, D., Sahar, T., Orr, S. P., & Pitman, R. K. (1998). Prospective study of posttraumatic stress disorder and depression following trauma. *American Journal of Psychiatry, 155,* 630 637.

Shalev, A. Y. (2000). Measuring outcome in posttraumatic stress disorder. *Journal of Clinical Psychiatry, 61* (5), 33 39.

Shear, M .K., Frank, E., Foa, E., Cherry, C., Reynolds, C., Vanderbilt, J., & Masters, S. (2001). Traumatic grief treatment: A pilot study. *American Journal of Psychiatry, 158,* 1506 1097.

Shulman, L. (1999). *The skills of helping individuals, families, groups, and communities,* (4th ed.). Itasca, IL: F. E. Peacock Publishers, Inc.

Simon, B. L. (1994). *The empowerment tradition in American social work: A history.* New York: Columbia University Press.

Sundet, P., & Mermelstein, J. (1996). Predictors of rural community survival after disaster: Implications for social work practice. In C. L. Streeter & S. A. Murty (Eds.). *Research on social work and disasters,* (pp. 57 71). New York: Haworth.

Turner, F. J. (Ed.). (1996). *Social work treatment: Interlocking theoretical approaches*, (4th ed.). New York: The Free Press.

Ursano, R. J., Fullerton, C. S., & Norwood, A. E. (1995). Psychiatric dimensions of disaster: Patient care, community consultation, and preventive medicine. *Harvard Review of Psychiatry, 3* (4), 196 209.

Weaver, H. N., & Wodarski, J. S. (1995). Cultural issues in crisis intervention: Guidelines for culturally competent practice. *Family Therapy, 22* (3), 213 223.

Weaver, J. D., Morgan, J., Dingman, R. L., Hong, B. A., & North, C. S. (2000). The American Red Cross disaster mental health services: Development of a cooperative, single function, multidisciplinary service model. *Journal of Behavioral Health Services and Research, 27,* (2), 14 18.

Weeks, S. M. (1999). Disaster mental health services: A personal perspective. *Journal of Psychosocial Nursing, 37* (2), 14 18.

Wells, R. A. (1994). *Planned short term treatment*, (2nd ed.). New York: The Free Press.

Woods, M. E., & Hollis, F. (2000). *Casework: A psychosocial therapy*, (5th ed.). Boston: McGraw Hill.

Zakour, M. J. (1996). Disaster research in social work. In C. L. Streeter & S. A. Murty (Eds.). *Research on social work and disasters*, (pp. 7 26). New York: Haworth.

Zinner, E. S., & Williams, M. B. (Eds.). (1999). When a community weeps: Case studies in group survivorship. Philadelphia: Brunner/Mazel, Inc.

References

American Psychiatric Association. (2000). *Diagnostic and statistical manual of mental disorders* (4th ed. Text Revision). Washington, D. C.: Author.

Armstrong, K. R., Lund, P. E., Townsend McWright, L., & Tichenor, V. (1995). Multiple stressor debriefing and the American Red Cross: The East Bay Hills fire experience. *Social Work, 40* (1), 83 90.

Armstrong, K. R., O'Callahan, W., & Marmar, C. (1991). Debriefing Red Cross disaster personnel: The multiple stressor debriefing model. *Journal of Traumatic Stress, 4* 581 593.

Barstow, D., & Henriques, D. B. (2001, December 2). Gifts to rescuers divide survivors. *The New York Times*, pp. A1, B7.

Bell, J. (1995). Traumatic event debriefing: Service delivery designs and the role of social work. *Social Work, 40* (1), 36 43.

Belluk, P. (2001, November 25). After Sept. 11, complaints of job bias mount. *The New York Times*, p. B6.

Belter, R., Dunn, S., & Jeney, P. (1991). The psychological impact of Hurricane Hugo on children: A needs assessment. *Advanced Behavior Research Therapy, 13*, 155 161.

Berenson, A. (2001, November 25). Will New York be told, once again, to drop dead? *The New York Times*, Section 3, p. 1.

Bertalanffy, L. von (1968). *General system theory: Foundation, development, application.* New York: George Braziller.

Bisson, J. I., & Deahl, M. P. (1994). Psychological debriefing and prevention of post traumatic stress. *British Journal of Psychiatry, 165,* 717 720.

Blair, J. (2001, November 11). In the aftermath of terror, grab a calculator and tally forth. *The New York Times,* WK p. 7.

Boudreaux, E. D., & McCabe, B. (2000). Critical incident stress management: I. Interventions and effectiveness. *Psychiatric Services, 51* (9), 1095 1097.

Burke, J. D., Moccia, P., Borus, J. F., & Burns, B. J. (1986). Emotional distress in fifth grade children ten months after a natural disaster. *Journal of the American Academy of Child Psychiatry, 25,* 536 541.

Burns, C., & Harm, N. J. (1993). Emergency nurses' perceptions of critical incidents and stress debriefing. *Journal of Emergency Nursing, 19,* 431 436.

Chemtob, C. M., Thomas, S., Law, W., & Cremniter, D. (1997). Postdisaster psychosocial intervention: A field study of the impact of debriefing on psychological distress. *American Journal of Psychiatry, 154,* 415 417.

Cohen, R. (1990). Post disaster mobilization and crisis counseling: Guidelines and techniques for developing crisis oriented services for disaster victims. In A. Roberts (Ed.), *Crisis intervention handbook: Assessment, treatment, and research,* (pp. 279 299). Belmont, CA: Wadsworth.

Conlon, L., Fahy, T. J., & Conroy, R. (1999). PTSD in ambulant RTA victims: A randomized controlled trial of debriefing. *Journal of Psychosomatic Research, 46* (1), 37 44.

Crossette, B. (2001, November 18). Unexpected guests warm hearts in the frozen north. *The New York Times*, p. A8.

Dembert, M. L., & Simmer, E. D. (2000). When trauma affects a community: Group interventions and support after a disaster. In R. Klein & V. Schermer (Eds.), *Group psychotherapy for psychological trauma*, (pp. 239 264). New York: Guilford Press.

Doka, K. J. (Ed.). (1989). *Disenfranchised grief: Recognizing hidden sorrow*. Lexington, MA: Lexington Books.

Donovan, A. (2001, November 4). In a suffering city, charity endures. *The New York Times*, pp. A33, A39.

Earls, F., Smith, E., Reich, W., & Jung, K. G. (1988). Investigating psychopathological consequences of a disaster in children: A pilot study incorporating a structured diagnostic interview. *Journal of the American Academy of Child and Adolescent Psychiatry, 27*, 90 95.

Ell, K. (1996). Crisis theory and social work practice. In F. Turner (Ed.), *Social work treatment: Interlocking theoretical approaches*, (4th ed., pp. 168 190). New York: The Free Press.

Ell, K., & Aisenberg, E. (1998). Stress related disorders. In J. B. W. Williams & K. Ell (Eds.), *Advances in mental health research: Implications for practice*, (pp. 217 256). Washington, D. C.: NASW Press.

Everly, G. S., Boyle, S. H., & Lating, J. M. (1999). The effectiveness of psychological debriefing with vicarious trauma: A meta analysis. *Stress Medicine, 15* (4), 229 233.

Finkelstein, K. E. (2001, November 23). Disaster gives the uninsured wider access to medicaid. *The New York Times*, pp. D1, D6.

Freud, S. (1961). The ego and the id. In J. Strachey (Ed. and Trans.), *The standard edition of the complete psychological works of Sigmund Freud,* (Vol. 19, pp. 3 66). London: Hogarth Press. (Original work published 1923).

Galea, S., Ahern, J., Resnick, H., Kilpatrick, D., Bucuvalas, M., Gold, J., & Vlahov, D. (2002). Psychological sequelae of the September 11 terrorist attacks in New York City. *The New England Journal of Medicine, 346* (13), 982 987.

Gammon, J., Daugherty, T., Finch, A., Belter, R., & Foster, K. (1993). Children's coping styles and report of depressive symptoms following a natural disaster. *The Journal of Genetic Psychology, 154,* 259 267.

Gist, R., & Woodall, S. J. (1998). Social science versus social movements: The origins and natural history of debriefing. *The Australasian Journal of Disaster and Trauma Studies,* retrieved November 12, 2001 from http://www.massey.ac.nz/~trauma/issues/1998 1/gist1.htm.

Golan, N. (1978). *Treatment in crisis situations.* New York: The Free Press.

Goldstein, E. (1995). *Ego psychology and social work practice* (2nd ed.). New York: The Free Press.

Goldstein, E. (1996). Ego psychology theory. In F. J. Turner (Ed.), *Social work treatment: Interlocking theoretical approaches,* (4th ed., pp. 191 217). New York: The Free Press.

Green, B. L., Grace, M. C., & Gleser, G. C. (1985). Identifying survivors at risk: Long term impairment following the Beverly Hills supper club fire. *Journal of Consulting and Clinical Psychology, 53,* 672 678.

Green, B. L., Korol, M., Grace, M. C., Vary, M. G., Leonard, A. C., Gleser, G. C., & Smitson Cohen, S. (1991). Children and disaster: Age, gender and parental effects on PTSD symptoms. *Journal of the American Academy of Child and Adolescent Psychiatry, 30,* 945 951.

Hepworth, D., Rooney, R., & Larsen, J. (2002). *Direct social work practice: Theory and skills* (6th ed.). Pacific Grove, CA: Brooks/Cole.

Hobbs, M., Mayou, R., & Harrison, B. (1996). A randomized controlled trial of psychological debriefing for victims of road traffic accidents. *British Medical Journal, 313,* 1438 1439.

Hoff, L. A. (2001). *People in crisis: Clinical and public health perspectives* (5th ed.). San Francisco: Jossey Bass.

Huerta, F., & Horton, R. (1978). Coping behavior of elderly flood victims. *The Gerontologist, 18,* 541 546.

Jacobs, A. (2001, November 13). A suburb pulls together for its grieving families. *The New York Times,* pp. B1, B7.

Kahn, J. (2001, October 14). Aid to the apple. *The New York Times,* p. 5.

Kershaw, S. (2001, November 24). Hard times in borough of airports. *The New York Times,* pp. D1, D2.

Kilijanek, T. S., & Drabek, T. E. (1979). Assessing long term impacts of a natural disaster: A focus on the elderly. *The Gerontologist, 19,* 555 566.

Kirst Ashman, K., & Hull, G. (1999). *Understanding generalist practice* (2nd ed.). Chicago: Nelson Hall, Inc.

Krug, E. G., Kresnow, M., Peddicord, J. P., Dahlberg, L. L., Powell, K. E., Crosby, A. E., & Annest, J. L. (1998). Suicide after natural disasters. *The New England Journal of Medicine, 338* (6), 373 378.

Kugel, S. (2001, November 11). Weeks of grief, then joy. *The New York Times*, p. CY 3.

Lee, J. A. B. (2000a). The empowerment approach to social work practice. In F. J. Turner (Ed.), *Social work treatment: Interlocking theoretical approaches*, (4th ed., pp. 218 249). New York: The Free Press.

Lee, J. A. B. (2000b). *The empowerment approach to social work practice: Building the beloved community.* New York: Columbia University Press.

Leonhardt, D. (2001, November 11). Troubled times for the whole world. *The New York Times,* p. WK 3.

Lewin, T. (2001, October 21). Shelters have empty beds: Abused women stay home. *The New York Times,* p. A16.

Lifton, R. J. (1982). The psychology of the survivor and the death imprint. *Psychiatric Annals,* 12, 1011 1020.

Lipton, E., & Johnson, K. (2001, November 8). Safety becomes prime concern at ground zero. *The New York Times,* pp. B1, B11.

Lyall, S. (2001, October 28). The terror prompts an outbreak of peace. *New York Times*, p. WK 3.

Margolis, O. S., Kutscher, A. H., Marcus, E. R., Raether, H. C., Pine, V. R., Seeland, I. B., & Cherico, D. J. (Eds.). (1988). *Grief and the loss of an adult child.* New York: Praeger.

Matloff, J. (2001, October 28). When a spouse is Muslim, new bonds, new rifts. *The New York Times,* pp. CY 4.

Mayou, R., Ehlers, A., & Hobbs, M. (2000). Psychological debriefing for road traffic accident victims: Three year follow up of a randomized controlled trial. *British Journal of Psychiatry, 176,* 589 593.

McKinley, J. C. (2001a, November 23). Albany slow to divide millions for charities. *The New York Times*, pp. D5.

McKinley, J. C. (2001b, November 24). Pataki paints by numbers to create dim picture. *The New York Times,* pp. D1, D4.

Miley, K. K., O'Melia, M., & DuBois, B. (2001). *Generalist social work practice: An empowering approach.* Boston: Allyn and Bacon.

Mitchell, J. T. (1983). When disaster strikes: The critical incident stress debriefing process. *Journal of Emergency Medical Services, 8,* 36 39.

National Association of Social Workers. (1999). *Code of ethics.* Washington, D. C.: Author.

National Center for Posttraumatic Stress Disorder. (2001, October 10). Effects of traumatic stress in a disaster situation. Retrieved March 29, 2002, from http://www.ncptsd.org/facts/disasters/fs_effects_disaster.html

New York State Office of Mental Health. (2001). Project Liberty: A Resource for Coping [Brochure]. New York, N.Y.: Author.

New York State Office of Mental Health. (2002, March 12). Project Liberty Services. Retrieved March 14, 2002, from http://www.projectliberty.state.ny.us

Nolen Hoeksema, S., & Morrow, J. (1991). A prospective study of depression and posttraumatic stress symptoms after a natural disaster: The 1989 Loma Prieta earthquake. *Journal of Personality and Social Psychology*, *61* (1), 115 121.

Norris, F. H., & Murrell, S. A. (1988). Prior experience as a moderator of disaster impact on anxiety symptoms in older adults. *American Journal of Community Psychology*, *16*, 665 683.

North, C. S., Nixon, S. J., Shariat, S., Mallonee, S., McMillen, J. C., Spitznagel, E. L., & Smith, E. M. (1999). Psychiatric disorders among survivors of the Oklahoma City bombing. *Journal of the American Medical Association*, *282* (8), 755 762.

O'Halloran, T. M., & Linton, J. M. (2000). Stress on the job: Self care resources for counselors. *Journal of Mental Health Counseling, 22* (4), 354 364.

Parad, H. J., & Parad, L. G. (Eds.). (1990). *Crisis intervention book 2: The practitioner's sourcebook for brief therapy.* Milwaukee, WI: Family Service America.

Phifer, J. (1990). Psychological distress and somatic symptoms after natural disaster: Differential vulnerability among older adults. *Psychology and Aging, 5* (3), 412 420.

Poulin, J. (2000). *Collaborative social work: Strengths based generalist practice.* Itasca, IL: F.E. Peacock.

Purdy, M. (2001, November 25). Bush's new rules to fight terror transform the legal landscape. *The New York Times*, pp. A1, B4.

Pynoos, R. S. (1992). Grief and trauma in children and adolescents. *Bereavement Care, 11* (1), 2 10.

Ragg, D. M. (2001). *Building effective helping skills: The foundation of generalist practice.* Boston: Allyn and Bacon.

Raphael, B. (2000). *Disaster Mental Health Response Handbook.* New Parramatta, New South Wales, Australia: The New South Wales Institute of Psychiatry.

Rappaport, J. (1990). Research methods and the empowerment agenda. In P. Tolan, C. Keys, F. Chertak, & L. Jason (Eds.), *Researching community psychology.* Washington, D. C.: American Psychological Association.

Rosen, J. (2001, November 18). Testing the resilience of American values. *The New York Times*, pp. WK 1, 4.

Ryan, K. (1999). Self help for the helpers: Preventing vicarious traumatization. In N. B. Webb (Ed.), *Play therapy with children in crisis: Individual, group, and family treatment,* (2nd ed., pp. 471 491). New York: The Guilford Press.

Saleebey, D. (1992). *The strengths perspective in social work practice.* New York: Longman.

Schwartz, J. (2001, October 28). Efforts to calm the nation's fears spin out of control. *The New York Times,* pp. WK 1, 2.

Sexton, L. (1999). Vicarious traumatization of counselors and effects on their workplaces. *British Journal of Guidance and Counseling, 27* (3), 393 403.

Sharkey, J. (2001, November 8). Holiday air travel is expected to be off sharply. *The New York Times,* pp. C1, C7.

Sheafor, B. W., Horejsi, C. R., & Horejsi, G. A. (2000). *Techniques and guidelines for social work practice,* (5th ed.). Boston: Allyn and Bacon.

Simon, B. L. (1990). Rethinking empowerment. *Journal of Progressive Human Services, 1,* 27 39.

Soliman, H. (1996). Community responses to chronic technological disaster: The case of the Pigeon River. *Journal of Social Service Research, 22* (1 2), 89 107.

Soliman, H. (2000). Generalist practice with survivors of natural disasters. In J. Poulin (Ed.), *Collaborative social work: Strengths based generalist practice,* (pp. 415 435). Itasca, Illinois: F.E. Peacock.

Soliman, H., & Poulin, J. (1997). Client satisfaction with crisis outreach services: The development of an index. *Journal of Social Service Research, 23* (2), 55 76.

Soliman, H., Raymond, A., & Lingle, S. (1996). An evaluation of community mental health services following a massive natural disaster. *Human Services in the Rural Environment, 20* (1), 8 13.

Soliman, H., & Rogge, M. E. (2002). Ethical considerations in disaster services: A social work perspective. *Electronic Journal of Social Work, 1* (1), 1 21.

Solomon, B. B. (1976). *Black empowerment: Social work in oppressed communities.* New York: Columbia University Press.

Solomon, S. D., & Green, B. L. (1992). Mental health effects of natural and human made disasters. *PTSD Research Quarterly, 3,* 1 7.

Steinglass, P., & Gerrity, E. (1990). Natural disasters and post traumatic stress disorder: Short term versus long term recovery in two disaster affected communities. *Journal of Applied Social Psychology, 20,* 1746 1765.

Steinhauer, J. (2001, November 23). City agencies are struggling with cutbacks. *The New York Times,* pp. D1, D6.

Stewart, B. (2001, November 18). Life in a hotel room: Home, cramped home. *The New York Times*, p. B9.

Taffel, R. (2001). From crucible to community. *Psychotherapy Networker, 25* (6), 23 24, 39 40.

Toner, R. (2001, November 18). Civil liberty vs. security: Finding a wartime balance. *The New York Times,* pp. A1, B6.

Tucker, P., Pfefferbaum, B., Nixon, S. J., & Foy, D. W. (1999). Trauma and recovery among adults highly exposed to a community disaster. *Psychiatric Annals, 29* (2), 78 83.

Weick, A., Rapp, C., Sullivan, W. P., & Kisthardt, W. (1989). A strengths perspective for social work practice. *Social Work, 37,* 350 354.

Wilgoren, J. (2001, November 25). Swept up in a dragnet, hundreds sit in custody and ask, 'Why?' *The New York Times*, p. B4.

Wright, K. M., Ursano, R. J., Bartone, P. T., & Ingraham, L. H. (1990). The shared experience of catastrophe: An expanded classification of the disaster community. *American Journal of Orthopsychiatry, 60* (1), 35 42.

Yalom, I. D. (1995). *The theory and practice of group psychotherapy* (4th ed.). New York: Basic Books.

Zastrow, C. (2000). *Introduction to social work and social welfare* (7th ed.). Belmont, California: Wadsworth Publishing Co.

Author Index

137

Subject Index